Mean Words

Helping your son stay strong in all-boy spaces

Mean Words

Helping your son stay strong in all-boy spaces

Copyright © 2025 Rob Pluke

Published by Courage to Connect

Cover design: Megan Pluke

Layout and typesetting: John Bertram, Tangerine Design

Queries may be addressed to pluke@polka.co.za

Contents

Introduction

Wired for relationship

The more I do this work, the more I see how deeply relational we are. We're so affected by other people. When we're with someone who loves and values us, we thrive. We feel happy and safe. We can relax. We can be our 'best selves'. But if we're with someone who criticizes us, or treats us as 'less than', we're likely to feel tense and upset. We could go quiet and withdraw, or we could find ourselves feeling defensive and hostile.

Of course, each relationship forms part of a wider network of connections, such as family, neighbourhood, workspace, or wider community. For better or worse, these groupings carry their own relational climate. And this climate, or culture, has a potent, pretty-much irresistible influence on its members.

This book focuses on a particular kind of community – the all-boys boarding school. It's a space I've come to know well. As a teen, I attended an all-boys boarding school, and now, as a consulting psychologist, I work within a fair number of boys' boarding schools in our area. So I know the terrain. I've seen the kind of impact 'meanness' can have, and I know some ways boys can better protect themselves from these effects.

Focusing on these kinds of schools allows me to be more detailed and nuanced in my advice. If you have a daughter, or your child doesn't board, or he's at a co-ed school, you will still be able to use almost all of the principles and techniques I describe. However, you'll need to tweak some of the finer details to suit your child and his/her school context.

I can't forget

I've seen him before. Now, some ten years later, he sits across from me, and the two of us get a welcome chance to reconnect, and look back over all that's happened in between. He's a really nice guy. Insightful, principled; with warm ways, and a ready smile. But he's here to talk about pain. And so, necessarily, the tone soon shifts from convivial to serious.

Fact is, I first saw him because, early on in high school, he'd been hurt, badly, by peer abuse. He was likeable then, and open-natured too. So he was easy to work with, and he soon went on his way – apparently fine. Now, in his early twenties, he realises the pain has never really gone away. Emotionally speaking, he still walks with a limp.

Together, we realise just how deep the wounding has gone. We see how his subsequent choices, both tiny and big, have been unconsciously slanted – away from pain and towards safer but smaller versions of himself. And this 'pain avoidance' and 'safety seeking' has become part of him. He's older, bigger, successful, and mostly happy. But deep down, he's still hurting. He hasn't properly healed.

Now as I say, he's a capable and pretty positive guy, so we were able to do some good repair and re-vision work. But honestly, his experience haunts me. I need us to see it; how much our school experiences can affect us, and how vulnerable we are to relational pain. So this book is for those boys and men, young and old, who've been damaged during their time at school. And this book is for parents whose boys are in (or soon to be in) boarding school.

Boarding school!

Over the past twenty years I've had the privilege of working with many wonderful boarding schools. There's so much to admire – the highly com-mitted staff, the amazing facilities, and the varied, often fun-filled days en-joyed by the students.

Yet as a consulting psychologist, I'm also very aware of the difficulties – both personal and organisational – that inevitably manifest when you have a lot of young people living together. A while back a Hospital Manager and I were talking about the need for an adolescent unit. He said *"Thing is Rob, I know there's a huge need. But to be honest, I'm reluctant. You just never know what they'll get up to"*. Working with young people can be tough!

Personally, I love working with teens. I love their energy, exuberance, and fresh insights. Still, I have to stay on my toes. Teens are in a state of flux, and things can very quickly shift. Sure, they're fun, but this can easily spill towards recklessness. And while there's often a lot of laughter, teens can also be irritable, moody, and best left alone for a while. So teens are great, but I can see why folk say they're not easy. And everyone has their stories.

It's a bit like that with boarding school. For some, boarding school conjures up images of austere buildings, aloof staff, and all manner of awful 'behind the scenes' goings on. Yet for others, boarding school signifies exciting opportunities, wonderful friendships, and important life lessons. Invariably, people have evidence for either side of the coin. They can tell you stories about people who've been either helped or harmed by boarding school. And quite often, folk are actually talking about themselves.

Now I don't think the pros and cons of boarding can be settled in any final way – too many variables are in play. Maybe the answer to the question: "Is boarding school good for a child?" will always be: "It depends…"

Key risk

Anyway, the merits of boarding are not the focus here. Rather, I want to zero in on a *key risk* of boarding: the damage that mean words, or peer meanness can cause. Very often, this is what makes boarding school unbearable. Very often, this is what 'bad side of the coin' stories are all about.

Some of this book explores the problem of meanness, and why it happens. But I think we need to accept that peer meanness happens at every school, and even good schools can't entirely extinguish the problem. If your child is at school, there's a very good chance he will experience mean words, at least to some extent.

So I want young people to know how to deal with, and properly recover from these experiences. They need to know, especially if they're boarders, because at boarding school, there really is nowhere to hide.

Long term benefits?

That said, the demands of boarding can teach a boy some vital interpersonal skills. Through boarding, boys learn how to fit in, and to get on, without losing themselves in the process. Boys learn to tolerate frustration, to live alongside difference, and to deal with conflict. Research confirms this; that the challenges of boarding can promote social and emotional 'agility' in a boy – capacities he can then take forward into adulthood.

However, this isn't always the case. If a boy is treated badly, and he doesn't know how to deal with the rough edges of all-boy spaces, then boarding will harm rather than build. So it's crucial for a boy to know how to deal with meanness, if it comes his way.

For every boy?

Some time back I met with a group of men – all past pupils (or Old Boys) of a particular school. Shared memories were the order of the day – some good, some bad, and some only realised in hindsight. In this vein, one of the men remarked: *"Shoo, we certainly weren't our best selves back then"*. He was struck by the careless ways they'd treated each other, and the regrets he carries to this day. I don't blame him though. It's not that easy to be nice at a competitive all-boys boarding school. When the pressure's on, and everyone's anxious about his standing, kindness usually drops away. 'Put-downs' become the order of the day.

As a result, the problem of meanness has both blatant and latent effects. Obviously, targeted boys suffer. But others are also affected. Meanness makes for a tense climate. More than one boy has told me he worries about becoming a target, and this worry changes how he acts. Even popular boys feel it. Everyone 'plays it safe' because no-one wants to be targeted. When meanness prevails, it's safer to keep your feelings to yourself. It's safer to pretend you don't really care. It's safer to like what everyone likes, and to laugh when everyone else laughs.

So I think every boy needs to understand meanness, and the impact it can have. I think it's good for a boy to reflect on the ways he might be shaping his choices under the threat of meanness; and who he's becoming in the process. I think it's good for a boy to work out, with people who love him, who he really is, what he really wants, and how to go about getting it. And I think it's good for a boy to feel equipped to deal with meanness even if, for the time being, he's dealing with an imagined fear rather than an actual experience.

Male spaces

As I say, this book focuses on the impact of meanness on boys. Much of what I say is relevant to co-ed spaces, to girls, and to girls who board. All the same, there are some important differences.

Studies show that:

- Boys hurt each other in ways that differ from girls
- Boy pain includes shame regarding issues of masculinity
- Boys are more likely to minimise their distress
- Boys are much less likely to talk about their pain

7

First Responders

I'll never forget, the one night, waking up, and realising someone was standing at the foot of my bed. I got quite a fright I can tell you. Then I saw it was James. He was just standing there, looking terrible, so upset. I said "Sweetheart, what's wrong?" and – oh gosh Rob – my poor boy just burst into tears.

Thing is, James hasn't been himself for quite a while – just not the happy chirpy guy he usually is. A day or so ago I asked him about it – I said "What's going on? You're not yourself these days. What is it?"

At the time he just said "Nothing", and now here he was. He said he couldn't sleep. He said he'd been thinking about what I'd asked. And then he told us what was going on at school. It was terrible.

But you know, at least now we know. At least we can help him. And I think to myself – sheesh, what if I hadn't asked him? What if we hadn't found out? It makes me go cold, just thinking about that.

As you read through this book, you may feel ill-equipped or a bit over-whelmed. You may feel like my advice is a bit technical, or that these kinds of problems are best left to a psychologist. Maybe. Sometimes.

However I want to assure you: for the hurting child, technical savvy is not the main requirement. Love is. Your growing, increasingly hairy, perhaps grumpy, son needs a safe place. He needs people who know him, and who are there for him through thick and thin. In other words, he needs you.

As his first responder, I want you to feel equipped. But remember, the most important aspect of my advice lies in the principle rather than the particular. In other words, once you get the gist of what I'm saying, you can apply it your way. You can be yourself, and use your own discretion, even with my advice in your mind.

The thing is, psychologists only see a very small proportion of boys, and usually only once they're really struggling. As an involved, informed parent, you can intervene way upstream, and end up avoiding more complex problems further downstream.

Summary

This is not an 'anti boarding-school' book. As we've seen, young people can learn a lot of life skills through boarding. However, if your son is to thrive, and make the most of his experience, he'll need to know how to deal with meanness. So we're going to take a close look at this problem. I want us to understand what it is, how it happens, and how to treat its effects. As parents and educators, we need to be able to appreciate the risk, so we can properly intervene and help young people recover.

Chapter 1

Soul Damage

When children are unhappy at boarding school, parents face a dilemma: should I push my child to stay, or do I yank him out, and look for a more suitable school? Lurking within the dilemma, giving it urgency, is the awful notion of 'damage'.

At times like these, parents say things like:

"Rob, is this going to damage my son? He says he wants to leave, but I keep telling him to hang in there, things will get better. But shoo, I'm so worried that I'm harming my son in the process!"

This is a really important issue. No-one wants this to happen to their child. But what causes damage? The answer to this question isn't that simple. Hardship and difficulty don't equal damage. Sometimes difficulty facilitates growth. Homesickness, whilst painful and distressing, doesn't necessarily cause damage. Strict rules and demanding teachers don't cause damage. Even school hierarchies, and new pupil rites of passage don't necessarily cause damage.

What does?

It's the way we're treated that causes damage. Instances of contempt and cruelty cause damage. These experiences can affect how we see the world, how we see others, and how we see ourselves. Being treated this way can change us, and our relational habits – for a long time to come.

This is borne out in trauma studies. When terrible things happen, we are far more likely to come through psychologically unscathed if our relational self remains intact. But if we are made to feel humiliated or denigrated during the ordeal, we are at much higher risk of traumatic injury. Such experiences can scar our souls.

Ordinary trauma

Peer meanness can be considered an 'ordinary trauma'. I know it's a strange and contradictory term. How can something traumatic ever be considered 'ordinary'? Well, this odd combination of terms conveys the following six truths:

1. Damage often takes place within everyday boarding school life.

2. As part of the 'ordinary', meanness is easy to overlook, deny, and dismiss.

3. Yet meanness can have a traumatic impact.

4. The sufferer is shamed.

5. The sufferer is drawn to blame himself for his wounds.

6. The damage can be lasting.

What does ordinary trauma look like?

1. *Walking out of chapel, pressed in by the throng, Jason feels a stinging pain in the middle of his back. Realising he's been slapped, Jason swings round, trying to identify the culprit. Everyone looks away. Some smile. But his attacker remains faceless.*

   A few minutes later, Jason walks into class. Keeping his head down, he makes his way directly to his chair. Just as he's about to sit, the person behind him pulls the chair back, and Jason almost falls.

2. *Walking into his dorm, Michael sees the rest of the group, clustered together, looking at him and smiling. He looks across at his bed, and he sees it's been flipped over... again. He loses it. He screams at the boys. "What's wrong with you guys? What have I done to you?" They watch. Some are smirking. Nick (always Nick), stands up. He's big. And he's intimidating. He walks towards Michael. "F... off, gayboy. No-one likes you. You shouldn't be here. Go on – phone your mommy. You always do." The rest of the group laughs.*

   Michael walks out, onto the fields towards the far end of the school. He doesn't know what to do. He will call his parents – later. But already he knows what they'll say. He can hear it now – "Come on Mike, just ignore them. It'll get better".

Such are the fleeting glints of menace within the everyday flow of boarding school life. They flash – then vanish, and all appears fine. Yet the impact remains. Internally, the sufferer is wounded. He experiences high stress, internal fragmentation, fear, guilt, shame, isolation, and sorrow. To adults it can seem relatively benign: just young people's silliness. But to the recipient, it can be devastating. I mean it. These kinds of experiences can change a child.

Why?

Relationships shape who we are. We often forget this. Perhaps because we live inside demarcated bodies, we assume a false independence from others. We forget the umbilical snip. We assume our thoughts, feelings, and choices are private, internal matters. All it takes, we think, is to 'stay positive!', 'take charge!', and set our own destinies. But it's not that simple. From the womb to the grave, we're profoundly affected – formed even – by those around us.

Again, we don't always realise this. But, as communal creatures, we all:

- have our realities defined by the larger social group we belong to. Whatever sits outside of 'group truth' is likely to be attacked or dismissed.

- internalize group habits and priorities. We learn what matters, and how life should be, and we enjoy validating feedback as we pursue recognised goals and interests. We feel happy and good, because we belong. The opposite applies if we are different or 'deviant' in our interests and goals.

- develop a shared sense of humour with 'our people'

- mimic facial expressions, postures, and mannerisms of our group (the chameleon effect).

- want to be seen as a 'good person'.

- dread being seen as 'deficient' or 'bad'.

- dread being rejected or ostracized. This is experienced as a kind of death.

This group effect is perhaps especially prominent in the adolescent years. It's very, very difficult for a teen to go against the grain, to accept that he's different, that he doesn't fit in with his peer group. A teen may take up a position of being different, and seem to be fine – proud even, of his stance. But invariably, this is a defensive position, because difference is so often cast as deviant. Consequently, being different usually includes a lot of internal stress and tension.

If teens experience social problems and are made to feel deficient, they will be affected in multiple ways. They will be affected at the level of:

The Heart

Feeling happy, and having a healthy sense of self, is not an individual achievement. It's not an internal commodity we cultivate on our own. In this sense, 'self-esteem' is a misnomer. It's not "I like me". It's "I am liked". It's 'me' in a 'self-other' relational field. Our confidence remains powerfully and profoundly fed by what others think about us. Am I worthy? Am I good enough? Am I liked? We can't determine this on our own. We need other people to confirm this. And we need pretty regular doses of approval.

Anyone who puts themselves out there needs feedback – "Was it good?", "Am I good?", "Am I loved?"

Again, this is not just for our kids. Just try being happy in a marriage where you're seldom appreciated, where your spouse doesn't seem to like who you are. You will be sad and stressed, and you'll probably get sick a lot. Or try feeling happy in a job where your boss is never satisfied, where you're always questioned, and doubted regarding your contribution. To say you'll be unsettled is an understatement. You'll be a wreck. You will dread going to work, and you're very likely to resign – for your own sanity.

In the same vein, any child who is shunned, criticized, teased, or taunted by his peers is at high risk of damage to his core self. Repetitive meanness will make a young person feel:

- guilty
- 'less than'
- highly stressed
- an inner sense of chaos
- weakened
- self-doubt
- self-criticism
- self-hatred
- ashamed
- sad or even depressed
- helpless
- hopeless
- anxious

The Mind

Even our thoughts are not really our own. Thought involves inner, imaginary dialogue with other people – spectres we're at best only half aware of. We all carry an internal sense of audience – often a critical audience – who judges what we say and do. So, we spend a lot of time explaining ourselves (to ourselves). We imagine our inner community of judges, and we defend and clarify how we see things and why we do what we do. We want to be seen as good. We dread the pain of being seen as 'bad' or deficient. Such thoughts – that we actually are bad or deficient, can torment us late at night. And teens can be especially susceptible to this – an internal self-critical voice, that's always there, just below the surface.

Also, as social creatures, we instinctively try to 'read' others' minds. We draw conclusions regarding how other people feel, what other people want and, crucially, what they think of us. When a boy is under attack, this capacity spikes. A boy tries to 'read' his social context, but because he's under threat, he makes all sorts of errors. He makes assumptions regarding how other people see him, and whether they like him or not. These are made rapidly, and they are usually inaccurate. Study after study shows our inclination to 'catastrophize' – to assume 'everyone hates me', and that there's no way to make it better. Such thinking can easily lead to crippling social anxiety and depression.

The Body

It's not just about how we feel and think. Relationships have a profound effect on us physically. Social pain and physical pain are processed by the same neurological system. When babies aren't held and touched, spoken to, and noticed, they get depressed. They lose weight, don't reach important physical milestones, and they can even sicken and die.

Of course we all get older. But the need for other people doesn't go away. We remain *very sensitive* to the ways we are treated. We all feel the pain of rejection, insult, or shame. When we're socially threatened, our inflammatory markers and blood pressure spike, and our immune system weakens. In contrast, feeling socially connected has powerful health benefits.

Even our postures – the ways we carry ourselves – change. Many years ago I worked with a youngster who'd been battling with peer difficulties during his junior school years. Then he moved on to a High School with a far warmer, more accepting social climate.

A few weeks in, I met his father, and he told me this story:

The other day I went to fetch my son from his new school. I waited for a while in the car park, looking around for my son, wondering where he was. I was a bit worried. He's usually so prompt. I thought maybe he'd forgotten where I said I would park.

Then I saw him – he was standing with a group of boys, and I hadn't recognised him at all! And then I realised – I didn't recognise him because, for the first time in ages, he was standing up straight!

Whole person

So meanness affects the whole person. If you want to know how your son is doing, look at his relational life. More than anything else, the quality of your son's interpersonal relationships gives you a window into his overall levels of well-being. Yet many boys suffer in silence.

The context

I must confess, I have an ambivalent take on boarding schools, especially if they're seen as 'good'. Again, there's a lot to admire – perhaps most especially the high quality staff who work with the boys. They give so much of themselves, in what tends to be an all-day and every day kind of job.

All the same, every organization has its 'shadow', and there are some downsides even to good boarding schools. If your son is struggling to fit in, we need to appreciate the contextual factors that could be adding to his stress.

Boarding schools tend to be big engines. They have their ways, and as a newcomer, you need to fit in. You have to yield to the way things work. Along the way, you are likely to absorb community frames of meaning regarding 'what matters' and 'who matters'. This can make good schools overly conformist, and antagonistic towards difference. Not amongst the teachers, but certainly amongst the boys.

All-boys boarding schools also tend to be performance-based, and competitive in nature. Again, teachers invariably have a healthy take on competition, but the boys often don't. Competitiveness feeds into hierarchy, and a better-than/less-than environment. Competitive spaces come with pressure – the pressure to achieve, *so that you can fit in and be accepted.*

Hierarchy leads to power disparities. This power can be formal (e.g. prefects) and informal (e.g. sporting or academic prowess). Power disparities can introduce an element of fear into the school. Many boys would much rather face an angry teacher than an angry, more powerful boy. When it comes to feeling happy at school, the opinions of peers matter more than the opinions of teachers. Teachers may be accepting and kind, but if your peers treat you as unacceptably 'different', you won't be happy.

Parents

We also have to look at ourselves, and the contexts we provide. Many boys sense how much the school means to their parents, and how invested we are in 'making it work'. Struggling boys often feel as though their parents are disappointed or frustrated with them for having peer difficulties, which makes things far worse. Of course, our sons can be wrong about this – they worry about disappointing us, when in fact we aren't disappointed at all, we're just worried.

I guess we just need to appreciate how much impact our expectations – real or perceived – can have on our sons. I'm not saying we shouldn't have expectations. We all do, and we should! But it can be difficult to know what to expect from our sons when they're struggling. What if your son is really unhappy, and it doesn't look like he's coping? What then? It's so hard to find the line between being too soft or too hard.

In the pages that follow, I describe some of the things I think we should ask of sons in these times. I want your son to know what you want from him, and why. I want you and your son to be on the same page, so as he starts to address his peer difficulties, he knows you've got his back.

A word or two about words:

Words are part of the fabric of relationships. From the womb, we absorb words, and they are integral to our closest bonds (Mitchell, 2000). Words have an impact. Especially mean words. Like a splinter, they can lodge in our minds.

Words carry both direct and indirect (relational) information. A simple phrase like "please pass the salt" has a two-level quality to it. Sure, it's about the salt. But also, through tone, timing and emphasis, the listener 'hears' how he's seen by the speaker. Does the asking convey approval and respect, or hostility and contempt?

This 'two level' feature partly explains why boys struggle to explain exactly how peers are being mean. Often, it's not so much what other boys say, as how they say it. If you miss this, you could make your son 'feel bad for feeling bad' – as though he's wrong or silly to complain because his peers aren't (on the face of things) actually saying anything mean. Of course, it's not what they say, but how they say it, that has the impact.

Words can also bring healing and growth. In the pages that follow, you will see that I want you to equip your son with strengthening words – things he can say (either to himself or to others) in the midst of his difficulties. Words can empower your son, and bolster his ability to contain the extremely distressing experience of being targeted.

Cyber words

Unfortunately, mean words can also be broadcast over social media. Simply put, this causes *significant distress*. It's one thing to be taunted in the moment, quite another when insults are posted, for all to see, *forever*. This magnifies, massively, a boy's sense of being scrutinised and scorned – a topic of gossip – an object to be mocked. There's no way to minimise it. Social media attacks are downright destructive. They can push a healthy, happy boy right over the edge.

A vicious cycle

Mean words can contribute to the following vicious cycle:

1. Hurt happens
2. In pain, the boy withdraws and/or becomes hostile
3. The boy is perceived as 'weird', or unfriendly, or disinterested
4. The boy ends up being avoided, even by nice kids
5. The boy 'mind reads' other kids, assuming global dislike and criticism.
6. The boy lives in a social echo chamber. He dwells on his hurt and isolation. Low in confidence and vulnerable, he becomes an easier target.

So hurt leads to fear, and fear leads to withdrawal and apparent unfriendliness, which then elicits social misreading, resulting in further hurt, mistrust, and isolation. Some of the angriest teens are also the loneliest, most defensive, and most inclined to self-sabotage. A boy can't be happy in this space. If he doesn't feel accepted, or that he belongs, his mental health will suffer.

It takes a pit-stop conversation to break out of the cycle. It takes a pit-stop conversation to restore a healthy sense of self. And it takes a pit-stop conversation for a boy to work out ways to navigate his social world. And for me, the person your son most needs to talk to, is you, his parent.

'The tongue has the power of life and death'
Proverbs 18:21

Chapter 2

Talking with your son

I want to keep this chapter as simple and as practical as possible. So what follows is a summary of what I do, with a little bit of explaining along the way.

What happened?

Before I offer any advice, I take as much time as is needed to bring what was done and said out into the open. As difficult as it may be, boy must talk about what happened if he's to properly heal. It's tender territory for sure, but I need to open up the wound, so the poison can get out. So I am both compassionate and direct in my approach.

I usually open by *saying "I'm so sorry you've had to go through this. I know how horrible it can be, and – to be honest – I'm amazed that you've coped the way you have* (I always look to build). *Bud, I know it can be difficult, but take a deep breath, be brave, and tell me what's been going on"*

Now with boys, I don't ask or encourage them to be vulnerable. Boys don't want to feel vulnerable. They already feel like losers. They already feel weak. I find it works better to say something like *"It takes a lot of courage to tell the truth. So try and be as brave as possible, and tell me everything. Try not to leave anything out"*. Right from the start, I'm looking to build into a boy in ways like these.

Nonetheless, your son needs to recount what happened. Social attack fragments the inner self. We go into a state of high alarm. We can't think straight. All our attention goes away from ourselves, and towards the threat. Physically, emotionally, and thought-wise, we go numb. We lose connection to ourselves.

If we don't get a chance to talk things through with someone, we stay disconnected. The incident remains unprocessed. It 'lives' inside of us, in its raw form, eliciting the threat response, and changing us from the inside – invariably for the worse.

Your first task then, is to help your child reprocess the incident. This helps to defuse the threat response, and your son can begin to re-integrate his selfhood.

What does this look like? Well, simply put, he needs to talk, and you need to listen. This is so important. Understanding provides the base for guidance. But more than that, 'feeling understood' is itself restorative. Even if you have little advice to offer, 'just' understanding does a lot. By putting what's been happening into words, your son is already on the road to reintegration. And if he can feel that you understand, then it'll be a lot easier for him to feel your support. He will feel your love and acceptance, and this will build him from the inside.

Good understanding also gives you a base from which to guide your son. Because you understand, you have a better idea of what he needs. So, before giving any advice, you need to know:

- what happened?
- where did it happen?
- when did it happen?
- who was there?
- what was said?

- what was done?

- who did/ said what? (tricky, because it can feel like 'snitching', but it's important)

- what was it like for your son? (How did hearing this, or having this thing happen, affect your son?)

Be wary of questions beginning with 'why'

You'll notice that none of these prompts starts with 'why'. Over the years I've noticed that 'why' questions (as in "why did that upset you?", or "why did they do that?") don't work that well. They tend to disrupt the flow of a boy's talk.

'Why' questions:

- inadvertently put your son on the back foot, as though he has to justify what he did or felt

- inadvertently change the conversation into an interrogation

- make your son more defensive, and less inclined to speak

- make your son more angry

- make it more likely for your son to say 'I don't know' (which is often, in fact, true. He knows what happened, but 'why' asks for reasons he can't think of).

- take your son away from simply recounting. Instead he has to take up a more analytical attitude towards his own experience.

- make your son think and talk in a more detached way.

- you will get thoughts rather than feelings

- the wound is less likely to manifest

- even if the wound does manifest, it will be less vivid, and easier to minimise

- make him feel like you don't understand

Look, it's not as if I never use the word 'why?' I do. But I've seen how, if I use the word *too soon*, boys tend to shut down. They say things like "I dunno", and I feel more and more like an interrogator. So here are some examples of the kinds of prompts I use (the possibilities are of course endless):

"Help me understand what's going on? "What happened?"

"When did this happen?"

"Where were you?"

"Who was there?"

"What happened next?"

"What kinds of things do they say?"

"Awful! What was the worst part of it?"

"Tell me more…"

"What was that like for you?"

"How do/did you cope?"

"What do you usually do when this happens?"

"Are there any good guys in the mix?"

Because…

Once boys start to talk, they do actually start explaining 'why' things happen as they do. But they get stuck. Due to complexity or first-blush thinking, they run dry. Now I want to help them think. I want them to develop their point of view. And I want to know how they see things, so I can be more helpful to them. So I use the prompt "because…?" It's a great substitute for "Why".

This is what it looks like:

Boy: I don't know… he says he's just joking… but I don't believe him…

Me: Because? (instead of 'Why')

Boy: Ah, it just… it just… like he's always putting me down. How can that be a joke? It doesn't feel like a joke to me anyway…

Me: What makes you say that?

Boy: Ah, well, it's like he's always gotta be better than me. He's always try'na keep me down. He can be nice, but when he's with the cool guys … it's like he's not my friend at all!

Me: You can't trust him?

Boy: Yes! One minute he's my friend, and then he's just a real jerk

By starting with what the boy says, opening it up and helping him to think further, two things happen. He gets a fuller understanding of the problem, and I get wonderful clues for further guidance and advice.

(Note: You could use the prompt "What makes you say that?". It works similarly to "Because". But I still prefer the prompt "because", as it's a softer, more seamless query.)

Search out the poison

A few boys can describe what's been going on, straight off the bat. But many struggle. Most hold what's happened in a no-go zone – especially the worst part! This zone is compressed with very uncomfortable feelings, beliefs, and body tension. In fact, in this zone, the whole self (mind, body, heart, and soul), remains locked and tense.

Very likely, as you come close to the wound, your son will say:

"I don't remember. To be honest, I don't really listen. I just try and ignore it (or forget about it), so I don't know what they say".

I say "Yes, but that's also because in that moment you were frozen. You couldn't think properly, so it's hard to remember". '

Now I know they kind of can remember. But this is the nature of traumatic material. One half of you works to forget about it, while another part of you carries it. Over time, it becomes an invisible burden – unrecognised damage – influencing us in profound and long-term ways.

So I need them to remember. To help them extract the poison, I give a few examples of the kinds of things I know boys target. I say something like:

"Yes, it can be hard to remember. Quite often, boys put someone down by saying something like... You're so... or "You've got ... "

And here are the usual target topics:

1. A boy's emerging masculinity ("You're gay" – this is a very common form of put-down. It denotes being 'other', inadequate, a failed male, and an object of scorn. If, as I suggest this, I see something register in his eyes, I might go on to suggest approximations of the same thing: "You're such a girl", "Pretty boy", "Gay boy").

2. A boy's physical self (the face, the head shape, body size, skinny or fat, clothing).

3. A boy's athletic self ("You suck; "You don't deserve to be in the team").

4. A boy's academic self ("What mark did you get?" *Said with derisive laughter).*

5. A boy's social self ("You've got no friends"; "You're such a suck up"; "What are you doing here?").

6. Non-verbal meanness (mocking laughter, turning away, hostile, cold, or contemptuous looks/grunts; rolling the eyes).

Giving boys opening prompts like these can make it easier for them to confirm and elaborate. In this way, the horrible experiences are 'spoken out', and contained by the relationship you share with your son. Also, and importantly, as your son elaborates, you start to get to the specifics of what he's been through.

Please bear in mind – the words can be crude, and difficult for a boy to share with his parents. They can sound like this:

"Prick"; "Pussy"; "You suck"; "Go kill yourself"; "You've got no friends"; "Why are you here?"; "You should leave the school"; "You don't belong here"; "You bring nothing to the school"; "Gay boy"; "You suck at…" "Your head/nose/ears look like …"; "Get your medication"; "You're ADD"; "Asperger's boy"; "You're bipolar".

Tears

Such words often have a catastrophic impact on the self, and if your son 'goes there' you are very likely to have tears. And your heart will break.

You will feel:

- very alarmed!

- very angry!

- so sad for your son

- let down (by the teachers/ school)

- your protective instincts will fire. You'll want to blast the threat away, defend your son, and help him feel better. One way of doing this is to knee-jerk into the 'reassurance route'. You could say things like: "they're just jealous", or "just ignore them".

- you might also go the protective/retaliatory route, saying something like "from now on, just have nothing to do with them!", or "I'm going to call Mr X, and give him a piece of my mind!", or "Next time, belt the living daylights out of him", or "Just kick him in the balls".

I get it, I really do. Unfortunately though, when it comes to social injuries, there are no 'justs'. To properly help our sons, we need to get into the details of their reality. We need to understand just how helpless they feel. We need to help them build authentic strength. We need to give advice our sons can actually use.

So slow down.

What else?

Once you and your son have gone through what's happened, take a moment. After a bit of time and silence, ask your son to stop and think again – to see if there's anything else he hasn't told you yet. Or anything he's had in his mind, but hasn't wanted to say 'til now.

I include this mostly because I know how hard it can be for boys to talk through their pain. And while they may allude to or hint at the kind of treatment they've received, they could well have glossed over a particularly hurtful, shaming experience – the one that really matters!

To get to this kind of confession, you could say something like:

"Bud, these situations can be really, really tough. Often, just thinking about it can make us feel really horrible, embarrassed, and ashamed. But please my guy, talk to me. I don't want you to leave anything out. Don't keep something stuck inside you.

So I want you to stop and think for a moment. Is there anything else that's happened that's been hard for you to say so far?"

At this, your son might describe more of what's happened. You get a more complete picture. If your son doesn't have much to add, or seems tired and 'done' with the conversation, you could say something like:

"Thanks so much for talking with me. I really appreciate it, and I know it can be hard. Bud, there may be things you haven't thought of now, or things that have been too hard to say. Please my guy. I love you. I want to be here for you. Give it some thought, and if there is anything else, please, please tell me. I'll check in with you later if that's ok?"

You might find that your son comes back to you – a day or two later even – to add more detail to this conversation. You could be driving in the car, and your son suddenly volunteers some new (perhaps awful) details he wasn't able to share at first.

This happens quite often – parents get told something really horrible, sometimes only years later. The good thing is, you can fast-track this process. You can help your son talk about painful things, off the base of the kind of conversation I'm describing here. He talks, and you listen. You've helped him to think, and you've helped him to 'go there' with you.

Finally, once your son has finished describing what happened, it can be helpful to ask him for a general comment about all that's happened. I ask for this kind of reflection because I want to know how a boy sees himself in context. I want to know whether he still feels like he can cope, or whether and how quickly school authorities need to be notified.

You'd ask:

"So bud, with all that's happened, where does all this leave you?"

OR

"When you look at it all, what does it make you think?

His reply will give his story an overall slant, or emphasis, showing you where he stands. His slant could be positive or negative.

Your son might say something like: *"You know, they can be good guys. It isn't always this bad"*.

This is an example of a positive slant. Here your son is wanting to calibrate what you've heard, so you don't go off the deep end. He's spoken about the bad but he's left out the good. When a boy says something like this, you know he mostly needs your support and advice rather than your intervention.

A negative slant example would be: *"Yeah, I don't know, I just don't know what to do anymore. I've tried everything. I think I need to leave"*.

This kind of general reflection shows your son is feeling defeated and overwhelmed. He could feel like he's at the end of his resources. He needs your assistance and your intervention.

Talk about shame

Once your son has described what's happened, take a moment to identify the distressing, embarrassing, fragmenting thing called *shame*. This refers to situations where your son has been made to feel inadequate, less than, an object of derision or scorn. He very likely won't use the word 'shame' or 'ashamed'. But as he talks, you will see the impact of the emotion-packed memory on his physical self – a flushing of the face, tears in the eyes, a downturn of the lips, and a tremor in the mouth. Whenever I see signs of it, I say:

"Bud, this is called shame. And, oh gosh, what a terrible feeling! I hate it! We feel so bad. We feel so stupid. We don't know what to do with ourselves. We feel like hiding away – like if the earth could swallow us up, it'd be a good thing!

But bud, we have to talk about it, because if we don't, this memory could haunt you for a very long time".

I talk about the fact that:

- shameful memories can keep us feeling bad about ourselves
- shameful memories can change us
- shameful memories can end up depressing us
- everyone, at some time or another, has felt shamed

This last point is important. I want a boy to know he's not alone. I want him to realize it's a case of "welcome to the human race". This serves as an antidote to shame, because shame is an ostracizing, 'I'm unacceptable' emotion. I might tell a boy about a time I felt shame. If I do, I also say how, each time I recount the story, I can still feel a bit of its poison.

What if your son won't talk at all?

Your son may simply not want to go there with you. For one thing, we instinctively try to not think about things that have shamed us. We want to forget – but we can't. So he could even dismiss the topic, and get angry with you for 'pushing' him to talk. He could say things like "Just leave it mom / dad. It was nothing. I'm over it".

One way of dealing with this could be to circle back later that day, and open up the topic again. Or you could wait for a reflective moment, like when the two of you are driving somewhere. Consider saying something like the following:

Hey Nick. Sorry my guy, but I'm your mom/dad, and it's kind of my job to worry about you (put the problem on yourself). It's just that I remember being teased / put-down at school, and it really hurt me. Actually, it knocked me back for a long time because I never told anyone about it. So I didn't deal with it properly. I kind of lost myself for a while. And I don't want that to happen to you.

Anyway, so I've been reading this book by this guy who says teasing makes us feel ashamed. He says shame does a real number on us. It makes us feel terrible, it really knocks our confidence, and it changes how we act around others. This is just what happens, because we're human (normalise shame).

So bud, you may not want to talk about it, but can I ask you to at least think about what it was like for you?

Cos lots of people get very tense inside (body). Lots of people feel like they can't even think straight (mind). And lots of people feel like they're stupid / no good, even though they know what the guy is saying isn't true (heart).

This guy says we feel a lot stronger if we talk about all this. He says words help us bring the gunk out into the sun, so we can start to heal inside. I want that for you. I want you to feel whole and strong inside.

So please think about it. And if you don't want to talk with me, maybe there's someone else you'd find it easier to talk with?

It's also worth remembering that asking good questions bears fruit even if your son won't talk with you. Good questions prompt thinking in a young person. He remembers what you've said – the way you've framed it. He mulls it over, and sooner or later he'll be more able to talk.

Reflect…

This chapter focuses on the importance of talking with our sons about social pain.

It's a difficult topic, so perhaps it's worth stopping to reflect….

1. Are you a family that opens up to each other?
   Score 1-10? Stories for evidence?

2. Are you a family that solves problems together?
   Score 1-10? Stories for evidence?

3. As parents, do you notice when your son is upset or hurting?
   Score 1-10? Stories for evidence?

4. Does he feel like he can talk to you?
   Score 1-10? Stories for evidence?

5. When your son does talk, does he feel like you understand?
   Score 1-10? Stories for evidence?

6. After talking with you, does your son end up feeling better or worse?
   Score 1-10? Stories for evidence?

Good communication and good relationships share a two-way street. You can't really have one without the other. So your relationship with your son needs to be in working order if you want him to turn to you and talk with you when he's struggling. I know this can be difficult during the teenage years, as lots of boys instinctively pull away from their parents, preferring greater privacy, and more time with their peers. This can be aggravated if your son is at boarding school, and he's not home all that much.

It was like that in our family. In my eldest son's eyes, there was certainly a season where my wife couldn't do anything right. For some reason, I was the good guy, and his mom was in the dog box. At the time I thought it was because I was the better parent – wiser perhaps, and easier to get along with. Yeah, right! When my youngest son hit the teenage years, it was suddenly my wife's turn to be the favoured parent, while I headed for the dog box.

So it just happens – this distancing thing – and it could be your turn to endure it. It's normal and healthy – *if our sons are happy*. But if they're unhappy, we have to draw close. If our sons are struggling, they need us, and we have to find ways to talk.

Talking about talking

If you and your son have a somewhat unstable relational/communication base, I suggest you start off by 'talking about talking'. It looks like this:

Nick, I know we haven't seen eye to eye recently. I've been on your case about homework, and I know it can be really annoying for you.

But bud, I can see you're not happy, and as your dad I can't just stand by and watch. Please my guy, tell me what's going on and I will do my best to listen and understand.

If you feel like I'm not getting it, or if you feel like I've slipped into 'lecture mode' again, just say the word 'dinosaur', and I'll do my best to keep quiet and just listen.

The above example is effective because:

1. You're working to describe the state of things between your son and yourself – from his point of view (step into his shoes)

2. You are *not* defending your side of the relationship (as in "I go on about your homework because I want you to reach your potential"). If you defend your side of things, your son will also stay on the defensive. Your goal here is to help your son drop his guard.

3. You do your best to describe the impasse between your son and yourself, acknowledging how your son might feel about that. Of course, he may correct you ("I don't get annoyed, I just get sad"), but this will be a *win* in terms of helping your son to talk.

4. You anticipate old habits that usually block your ability to listen to each other, and you find ways to get around them ("If you feel like I've slipped into lecture mode...")

5. You stay humble. You take the 'one-down' position as a way of defusing hostility. This is not a time to be 'in charge'. This is a time for closeness. For support. For thinking together to find a way forward. Remember, part of your son's anger and defensiveness is being fed by hurt and helplessness. So step down, and tend to his wounds.

Be reassured; times of crisis can be opportunities for renewed closeness between parent and child. It's just that if the relationship is strained, then 'talking about talking' will need to happen first. And the more unstable the relationship is, the more 'talking about talking' you'll need to do.

No secrets

Trust me, when a bunch of young people stay together, a lot of weird stuff can happen. And some of it can be nasty. So I'd encourage you to set up a 'no secrets' agreement with your son. Find an opportunity to ask your son to *promise* he will tell you if something is upsetting or hurting him. Again, I know he's not at home. And he's a boy. But he's your boy. And if he's struggling, he needs you.

It could also be good to ask your son if there's anything about you as his mom or dad that would make it hard for him to confide in you. To be honest, quite a few things can stop boys from confiding in their parents, but from what they tell me, these are the top reasons:

1. You'll stress too much.

2. You'll only make things worse.

3. You'll just say….

4. You'll get angry.

5. He doesn't want to disappoint you.

6. You're too busy, or too preoccupied.

7. You won't listen, or take him seriously.

Each of these possible reasons contains fairly dense relational material, regarding possible blockages between you and your son. So, if he hints at any of the above, it will be worth taking some time to discuss the implications this carries regarding your overall relationship with your son.

Summary

Ok, so your first step is to get a good grasp of what is. This is already healing for your son. By 'just talking' and having you to witness his pain, you've helped your son access his true, inner self. And he's done this with you – someone who knows who he is and who loves him through and through. In the process, he's started to think with greater awareness – about himself and about his situation.

With this base in place, you are now able to equip your son with concrete skills – things he can do and say when he finds himself in difficult or threatening peer situations.

Chapter 3

What should I do?

People aren't direct. People don't just come out and say what's annoying or upsetting them, or what they actually want. So if your son has been struggling socially, he'll sense that boys don't seem to like him, but he probably won't really know why or what he should do to fix it. This causes high alarm. It's the uncertainty that kills. Not knowing leads to gloomy self-reflections and conclusions:

"Why me?"

What am I doing wrong?"

"I'm not good enough!"

"There must be something very wrong with me!"

Again, it's the vagueness that destabilizes us. Put-downs elicit distress – not enlightenment. In his distress and confusion, your son will recoil. Very likely, he will try to make himself small. He may also resolve to never again do the things that seem to elicit scorn.

Not doing something isn't bad. Even loving parents give 'don't do' advice – "don't shout out", or "don't argue back", or "don't show them you're upset". This can be helpful, but it has to be linked to the kinds of things our sons *should* do. If a boy shouldn't shout out or argue back, what should he do instead? What new way fills the vacuum?

The inner/outer self

In terms of 'new ways', I have two main goals in mind. First, I want a boy to restore his sense of self. And second, I want him to build his interpersonal skills.

This may be thought of as working on the inner/outer self. Perhaps obviously, these two 'selves' complement each other. As you stabilise your inside self, your outside self becomes more skilful. And vice versa.

This inside/outside dynamic is the relational field you are working in, the field you're looking to explore, come to understand, and up-skill. You can use the diagram below to talk about the 'inside/outside' self with your son:

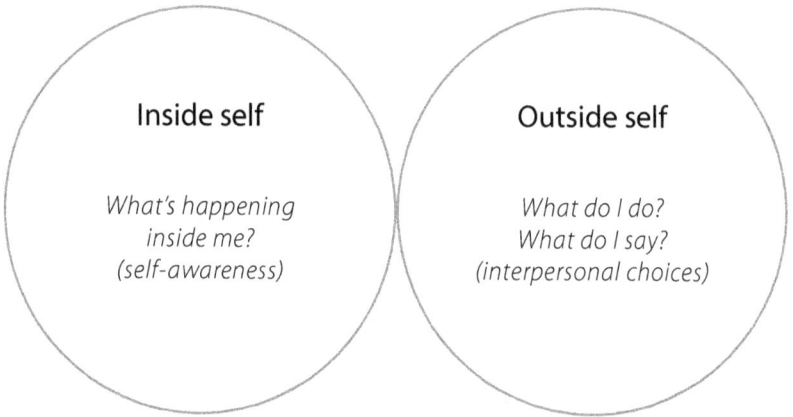

Inside self

*What's happening
inside me?
(self-awareness)*

Outside self

*What do I do?
What do I say?
(interpersonal choices)*

The inner self

I almost always start off by focusing on the inner self. I know the person in front of me faces a whole lot of problems 'out there'. Yet I also know he first needs to learn how to contain all the distress he experiences. And he needs to get better at thinking in the heat of the moment.

Help your son stay centred in the storm

Focusing on the physical impact of mean words is a crucial early step. If your son doesn't learn to watch and contain his physical self, he's more likely to get and stay tense. This will change his moment-by-moment choices. Because he's in 'danger mode', he's more likely to over-react, shut down, or hide away. His very posture – the way he carries himself – will change. He will look small, hesitant, and weak, or tense and defensive. Consequently, he will draw more attention from bullies.

The problem is, the body responds to mean words the same way it responds to other kinds of danger: by activating the sympathetic 'fight, flight, or freeze' response. We can't think properly, our hearts race, our muscles tense; our breathing changes – even stopping for a few moments. This is involuntary, so gaining some measure of physical calm can be tough!

However, I don't need your son to completely *relax* when he's under fire – that's unrealistic. What I want is for him to practice staying *centred in the storm*. This is not really about relaxing – being calm. It's about staying connected to what is actually happening in the body. It's about noticing inner tension, noticing fear, and continuing to think. It's about waking up – stepping out of shame-induced numbness – so you can make good choices.

With this in place, your son will be better able to look after himself when he's under fire. He will be able to hold his dignity. And, he'll be more able to notice social cues. In other words, he'll be more able to read other people.

If we're physically disconnected, we're relationally disconnected. What I mean is, the less we know about what's going on 'in here' (the body), the less smart we'll be about what's going on 'out there' (with others). This is especially the case in conflict situations. The more stressed we are, the more our focus narrows, the more we're likely to react or shut down in non-creative ways. We will be locked into the vicious cycle of fight, flight, or freeze described above.

So before your son goes out there again, he needs to learn how to stay centred in the storm. I usually begin by saying something like:

"Bud, you might not actually realise it, but oftentimes you're stuck in threat mode. I really don't blame you – at all – because I know how hard things can get out there. What do you think of what I've just said? Do you realise this?"

I start off this way because a lot of boys are in the fear zone, but they don't know it. Their focus is on what's outside of them – the threat 'out there'. I want them to focus on themselves, starting with the ways their bodies are triggered by danger. Sometimes I draw the following diagram, to show boys where their bodies are likely to be activated.

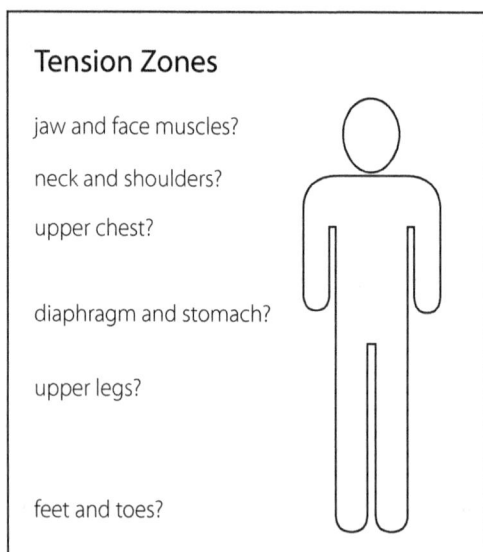

Tension Zones

jaw and face muscles?

neck and shoulders?

upper chest?

diaphragm and stomach?

upper legs?

feet and toes?

Take a moment to discuss this with your son. If he recognises where he gets tense, he can practice 'unlocking' those muscle groups during the course of his school day.

If I had to pick two areas to focus on, it would be 'coat-hanger shoulders' and a 'jelly belly'. I say *"Think of a coat hanger, and how its arms go down. This is how I want your shoulders to go. Imagine hanging your shoulders on a coat hanger. At the same time (placing my hands on my diaphragm) make this part of you soft – like jelly".*

Then I'd ask my son to picture his antagonists, imagine them looking at him, and speaking in hostile or cutting ways. And, with that image in his mind, I'd ask him to release physical tension in his shoulders and his belly. This will probably feel strange – even wrong. We're not wired to relax when threatened. But again, it's about being centred rather than completely chilled.

I'd also ask him to practise holding a good posture – to stand tall, shoulders back, head up, and his face open. This makes more difference than we realise. Standing tall elevates testosterone and suppresses cortisol production. When people stand tall, they feel more in control, more confident and positive. On the other hand, when we 'close in' on ourselves, and make ourselves small, we're more prone to feeling anxious, overwhelmed, and depressed.

Now I know, anyone who's under fire isn't going to be relaxed – but it will be great if he can stop fragmenting, remember to breathe, relax his shoulders, and *think*. This is really important. It will help your son towards building a personal shield that can protect him from mean arrows.

Help your son find his anchor statement

Self-talk is also important. Intentional, or deliberate self-talk activates the prefrontal cortex, which helps your son cope with difficult feelings, and make no-regret choices. Healthy, intentional self-talk can re-orientate your son, and give him better, wiser understanding of the situations he finds himself in. Intentional self-talk can work as a kind of internal personal shield. It can help your son feel more integrated, more settled, and more confident in himself.

This is especially important in difficult or distressing situations. What can your son say to himself when he's taking strain, or being treated badly? It certainly doesn't have to be fancy. Brené Brown, an expert on shame, describes how a friend says the word 'Ow!' when she feels shamed. In this simple way, she turns to herself with compassion and awareness, which then helps her to more quickly find her feet.

In the same way, I want your son to have one thing he can remember, or say to himself, to break out of the shame state. I call this an 'anchor statement'. It's not a clever come-back. It's not about confronting one's antagonists. It's about turning toward the self with compassion, and remembering, or protecting, one's personhood. To me, this is way more important than a snappy comeback. The thing is, social life is fast and fluid, and it's not always easy to know what to say to others. Sometimes, returning fire is good, and sometimes staying silent is better. You never know until it happens. So for me, retorts are optional. But self-statements are not.

Also, many boys aren't good at comebacks – it's just not in their natures. This is especially the case with boys who are targeted. In some ways they're easy prey partly because they aren't good with comebacks.

An anchor statement can unfreeze your son's mind, and help him stay composed in the heat of the moment. It can help him feel stronger in himself, so he can be more creative in tough spaces. Remember, teasing makes us an object of evaluation – caught in the spotlight of the group gaze. This potent negative experience needs to be undercut. You want your son to think clearly and healthily in the midst of that difficult moment.

However, it requires a bit of reflection. First, you need to find out, more or less, what your son 'says' to himself in those moments. Now, my guess is that if you asked your son what he was thinking at the time, he'd say *"I don't know"*, or *"Nothing"*. This is because normal self-talk is not intentional. It's more of a subconscious mental state, than actual words. We have to take a bit of time to work out the words to describe our inner state. So, on reflection, your son might realise that when he's teased, he 'says' to himself: *'I'm a loser'*, or *'I'm alone'*, or whatever.

This knowledge will show you what kind of anchor statement your son needs. What self-statement could serve as a remedy to his real-time pain? Please check this with your son, as he's the one who needs to use it.

A while ago I was talking with a young boy who was really struggling with boarding. He *said "My parents tell me 'think like this – think like that'. They say 'Jason, you must be strong'. But in my head I tell myself 'No I can't do this'. And I just feel worse"*. The problem here is that Jason's parents hadn't accessed his actual mental state ('I can't do this'). And, with all the love in the world, they were trying to get him to feel something he couldn't feel. Jason was feeling terrible. He was feeling weak. So, inadvertently, encouraging him to be strong was making him feel even more of a failure – even further from the required mark.

Now I know you love your son to bits, and you desperately want him to remember his priceless worth. There may be all sorts of things you want him to remember. The problem is, when your son's in a battle zone, he won't be able to feel amazing or great about himself. And he won't be able to remember a long sentence.

Remember, the goal of the anchor statement is to unfreeze your son, to centre him, and to help him think more clearly in difficult spaces. So keep it simple, direct, and down to one word if possible.

Your son might like the example given by Brené Brown (*"Ow!"*).

Some boys have liked:

"Thanks!"

Or

"Whatever"

As internal statements, 'Thanks!' and 'Whatever' can be said in a range of ways, according to how your son feels at the time, so there's an emotional resonance there. The words also establish your son's dignity, while unsettling the antagonist's position. A further advantage is that both words are pretty effective as quick, non-combative retorts your son could actually say to another boy, when the time is right.

One boy liked the word *"Core"*

He used the word as a prompt to check in with himself at the level of the diaphragm or belly. To me, it was both a physical and a self-honouring/spiritual act. At the time, I placed my hand on my diaphragm and said, *"No matter what those guys say, don't let it into this part of you. Remember who you are. Make contact with this part of you, with just your mind, and say the word 'core' to yourself"*.

Another boy also practiced focusing on his core, while holding the words *"You got this"* in his mind. Our conversation went like this:

"So bud, when you feel the hit, just send your attention to your inside – here" (placing my hands on my diaphragm, I blow out a burst of air) *"Whooo!"*... *"You got this!"* .... *"It's just a flash, but then you've got your base"*

"Ok. It's like an acknowledgement".

"Yes, it's like an acknowledgement".

I saw him again a week later, and our conversation went like this:

"I've been trying that thing you told me, and it's been helping"

"Oh yes? Tell me about it"

"Ah well, if I pick up something, that I perceive is towards me, I look upwards, close my eyes, take a breath, and say 'Ok that hurt a bit'. Then I just relax my body and carry on doing what I was doing."

"And that helps?"

"Yeah, it's like it defuses things. As it comes over, it doesn't build up like it used to. It just passes out. There's not a build-up of uh, suppressed – like – feelings. Like I'm not so irritable, or inclined to snap if they do something."

"Has it been easy to remember?"

"I think the more I use it – like every time I come across a situation, it's like the first thing that pops into my head. It's becoming second nature, subconsciously, I guess."

Interestingly, what this real-life example shows, is that it's not the words that really matter – it's the compassionate turn towards the self. The idea, after our first session, was that he'd use the words 'you got this'. But he didn't! Instead, much like Brené Brown's friend, he turned to himself with simple words of self-acknowledgement.

Look, I'm glad I gave him the encouraging phrase "you got this", and I think it's somewhere in the mix of his real-time strategy – my vote of confidence in him. So words do matter, but only insofar as they raise self-awareness. Help your son find words to contain what is, rather than where you think he ought to be.

What works for you?

Of course, it's always better to pass on something we've already tried out for ourselves. So what's worked for you? I sometimes tell boys how, as a teenager, once a year, I had to visit some difficult 'put-down' type relatives. They really used to get under my skin, and then I'd be out-of-sorts for the rest of day.

But after a while, I started to think more objectively about their ways. You could say I 'decoded' their strategies. I also spent some time speculating on the reasons why they did what they did – the personal issues, underlying insecurities or wounds they perhaps carried. Happily, this protected me from their discouraging ways. When they did their thing, I'd still feel the hit, the difference being, I could *recognise* it. And, with an internal smile, I could say *"There it is"* to myself.

That was all it took. I didn't always remember to do it, but when I did, this simple strategy gave me the self-other objectivity I needed to keep my balance. This gave me strength, and actually helped me to keep loving them, despite their vexing ways.

Presence

As I say, it's not only the words that make the difference. An anchor statement also signifies 'presence'. The words signify a turning towards ourselves – a moment of self-recognition – which can really help in the heat of the moment. And, if you take time to 'decode' the other boy's actions without condemning him, then you also promote 'other recognition'. Perhaps then, in time, your son might also be able to smile inside when he faces meanness, because he's able to be more present – more self and other aware – in these difficult moments. His antagonist will become less imposing, less 'all-powerful', and your son will feel less helpless, less frozen.

Importantly, there's also you, his parent. Because your son has come up with these words in conversation with you, he's not as alone. Even as he uses the words, he remembers you. He has an impression or sense of you in his mind, and the sound of your voice, saying these very words.

This is especially the case if you've *taken the time to understand*. Because you understand – because you've resonated with your son's pain, whatever you say has power. You can say something like, *"Sheesh bud, this is hard. If it happens again, just think of me. Think of this chat now. When you see it, you'll know – that's it! That's exactly what Dad and I were talking about.*

My guy, you know how much I love you. You know how proud I am of you. So just think of me – of us – in those moments. I've got your back. And remember our saying 'Never alone!'".

The body, then the mind

Usually, I combine the above strategies into one conversation. Even as I'm showing a boy how to centre his physical self, I ask him to practice holding an anchor statement in his mind. Nevertheless, there is a sequence to it, because a boy can't hold onto an anchor statement if he's too distressed. So calming the body – learning to centre the self in the middle of a storm – is where you start. *You turn to the body to quiet the mind.* This physical 'felt sense' is your son's primary base. In fact, if I had to pick one strategy for dealing with mean words, this would be it – learn to calm the self in the face of meanness.

It's not easy though! For many boys, it takes time to develop this skill. So don't rush it. Don't suggest a whole lot of higher order strategies to your son until he's learned to calm his centre. Signs that your son isn't there yet will be things like:

- You're giving advice and you notice your son has a detached, 'thousand yard stare'

- You're giving advice and your son gets very tearful and distressed

- You're giving advice and your son gets angry and starts to yell

- In his distress, he says things like *"It will never work!"* or *"I've tried all that!"*

It's difficult. We want our children to be happy. We want their problems to be solved. We want the meanness to end. Yet we mustn't rush. We must give our sons the time they need to settle themselves, so they can properly think, and begin to problem solve with us.

Fused

The thing is, your son could be feeling really stuck, or completely caught up by his problems. Some psychologists would say he's in a state of fusion.

He's entangled in his distress. He can't think properly, or look beyond his problems. This is where the above exercises come in. They help your son to take a step back, and to think. As your son sends a spoke of awareness to his belly, or the tension in his chest, he starts to defuse. Added to this, he begins to fix his mind on some higher order, orienting thought. This gives him direction, and helps him to access his more effective, preferred self.

Try it yourself. The next time you're in busy traffic, or someone cuts you off, try sending a spoke of awareness to your diaphragm. You could even say ""Thanks!" or ""Thanks a lot!" and see how that makes you feel. This will give you a felt sense of what you're asking your son to do. You'll probably find that you're less likely to yell, or to make some impulsive 'I'll show you' manoeuvre. And, as a bonus, you'll be protecting your adrenal glands, and saving your energy for things that really matter.

Late night musings

It would be great if your son could practice some version of this 'body-mind' re-set before he goes to sleep at night. I have a couple of reasons for suggesting this. For one thing, if he's going to practice, then this is a good time to do it. He's in his bed. He's starting to unwind, and this body-mind sequence can help him towards a good night's sleep. He relaxes his body and he remembers *"Never alone..."* Again, I think there's a spiritual aspect to this. It's like a meditative prayer at the very tail end of the day.

But I also suggest this practice because I know that targeted boys are very prone to late night fretting. This is when they're visited by stressful or depressing thoughts. This is when feelings of shame and sorrow cast their longest, darkest shadow. A healthy, intentional self-statement, coupled with a softening belly, and calming breaths, can break the spell. It can serve as a lantern to the soul, reminding your son that he is not alone, that he is loved, and of the hope that lies ahead. This is the kind of base your son will need, if he's to try new things in the world 'out there'.

Chapter 4

Strategies for the world out there

Now it's time to equip his outside self. You've helped your son boost his self-awareness and acceptance. Now he needs to look at ways he can get stronger 'out there'. This keeps hope and optimism alive. Your son needs to feel like he is growing, getting better, and getting stronger. Right now, things may be bad. He might feel isolated and stuck. But if he's willing, he can grow.

It's just that strength must happen from the inside-out. Your son needs to stay close to the truth of what's going on inside of him even as he responds in new ways. If he's an introvert, he's an introvert. But he can still grow. He can still learn new skills, become more resilient, and more able to deal with meanness.

This is called *response flexibility* and it's a key ingredient of effective adult living. Response flexibility involves

1. knowing what I'm feeling (the truth of what's going on inside of me)

2. containing what I'm feeling (centring the self)

3. responding in creative and effective ways

So it's about having a feeling, but choosing your response. This is powerful. Response flexibility frees you up to live your best life, despite adversity. It requires practice, but it's crucial! If we let bad feelings and setbacks dominate, our only options are to keep ourselves small, to withdraw and to avoid.

So even if your son is in a very difficult time right now, he must begin to focus on everyday choices. These choices will help your son feel more in control. And he can be authentically proud of himself for taking these steps. All the preceding steps prepare your son for brave action. You've helped him to talk about what's been happening. You've helped him speak about his pain, and the awful experience of shame.

You're also helping your son to centre himself in the storm, and to set his mind on his anchor statement. These are already creative steps. These actions are already making for response flexibility. Under attack, he relaxes. He remembers to breathe. His mind is racing, but in the midst of the blizzard, he recalls his anchor statement – his truth. *That's response flexibility right there!*

But it's not enough. Your son also needs to be taught optimal ways of entering into social spaces, and he needs to feel equipped to deal with meanness.

Here are my top 'outer self' strategies:

Be a good guy

This is more than a strategy. It's an overall attitude – a way of being, an inner ethic, and a way of relating: be a good guy. As simple as that. I know it sounds a bit insipid. Yet when it comes to making and keeping friends, it works.

Aiming for status – being important – also works. It's a quick route to popularity, and it comes with a lot more bling, so a lot of boys go this way. They strive for recognition. They strive to be good at something, or to get buff, or to be part of the cool group. It's so seductive. Yet as studies show, in the long term, it doesn't actually work. Mitch Prinstein says aiming for status – trying to be important – engenders more stressful, competitive social spaces. Going this way is fraught. One minute you're up, the next you're down. Your value hinges on your performance, so you can never really rest. Boys who go this way can lose touch with themselves, and often end up feeling empty inside.

Prinstein says it's far better simply to be 'likeable', or in our terms, a 'good guy'. It's not flashy. You don't always stand out. But over time, other boys are drawn to your down-to-earth friendliness. They feel safe with you. They like and trust you. You're just a good guy.

Boys don't always see this. A Grade 8 boy once told me how struck he was by a senior boy's school blazer. It was festooned with badges of honour, and this youngster dreamed of one day having a blazer just like that. I get it. I don't want to take his ambitions away. Still, we have to resist the siren call of status. Going that way can change us. We can forgo our better qualities. We can forget to enjoy ourselves and the people around us, because we're too driven – too hungry for success.

Keep faith in the small moments

Now if your son is dealing with put-downs, being made to feel 'less than', he might start to see high status, or 'being important', as his only way out. Yet it won't work. So help your son stay grounded. Remind him what 'winning' actually looks like in social terms. Help him to look again at himself, his deeper values, and then to think of every-day ways he can be a 'good guy' out there in the world. It's not about being 'all that'. It's about the small moments. In the boarding house, during the school day, and on the sports field. How can he go about fostering good social connections? Who can he compliment or encourage? What should he do and what should he say? Where? When?

And who are the other good guys? Who should he draw close to, or align with? Building connection with one or two 'good guys' in a group helps keep hope alive. It helps your son feel more positive about himself and his world, making it less likely he'll lose it, or lash out in anger when the arrows come his way.

More than once a boy has told me how he's turned things around just by being nice to the boys in his group. When I press him to explain, I tend to get pretty vague replies. But reading between the lines, I see it's been about deliberately stepping into friendliness and laughter. It's been about taking up an attitude. Then, from this attitude, 'good guy' ways happen automatically.

Importantly, 'being a good guy' is founded on healthy self-regard. You want your son to move into a space where he sees everyone in the group, including himself, on equal terms. It's not one-up/ one down. It's same-as. So perhaps before your son can be a good guy, he needs to know how to centre himself, dissolve the shame state, and remember his inviolable worth.

'Be a good guy' is my first strategy for the world 'out there'. It serves as a constant. Even when a boy is really battling, or facing a lot of group heat, I encourage him to keep faith in 'being a good guy'. Along with this I do a lot of inner-self strengthening. But I consistently aim for two things: (1) get out of the shame state, and (2) keep being a good guy.

If your son can hold onto this twofold self and other attitude (self and other – honouring), he will prevail! It may take time, but it will work. Also, with this in place, he will be more able to deploy the skills that follow. Carrying this 'felt sense', or inner orientation, will help him remember what he stands for and what he's calling others to. Knowing and remembering goodness can give him an inner conviction. It also serves as an excellent base for the following, proven, social strategy.

Social Judo

I use this term because what looks like yielding is in fact winning. You go with your adversary's force or momentum. It's based on the above strategy (being a good guy), and it's one of the best ways of actually building bonds in the midst of meanness. It takes a fair amount of practice – no-one gets a black belt straight away – but it can be very effective once you get it.

This is what it looks like:

Tormentor: "You suck at Tennis!"

Son: "I know! I've got so much to learn! That's why I practice so much. How did you get so good?"

There's a lot of skill and strength in this kind of rejoinder. For starters, you have to roll with the punch. Take the hit and keep smiling. You admit you're not the world's best Tennis player. But you also back yourself. By saying something like 'I've got so much to learn', you keep faith in your ability to get better.

Then, you complete the masterful Judo throw by *complimenting your adversary!* This is akin to Kalman's idea of turning 'bullies into buddies' – disarming bullies through calmness, self-acceptance, humour, and generosity. Through his program, Kalman seeks to teach young people to avoid losing strategies such as anger and quick retaliation, and to take on 'friend – building' ways of responding.

Now I know this is a bit of an emotional flick-flack – complimenting someone who's mean to you, someone you're actually afraid of. But it's actually a very powerful way to turn a nasty guy around, and get him to soften his ways. Generally speaking, people – even pretty tough guys – respond positively to sincere and accurate compliments – being noticed in an affirming way.

Of course, every situation is different. But what stays constant is your son's down-to-earth self-acceptance, and his ability to invite his tormentor towards goodness. It certainly doesn't have to be fancy. One boy, when told that he 'sucked at football', simply responded, *'Thank you!'* His chirpy, upbeat comeback completely befuddled his tormentor, who never bothered him again.

It could take your son quite a while before he's able to use this skill. You might need to restore his base of self-acceptance and worth. You might need to remind him what 'winning' looks like socially. Your son will also need to know how to stay centred in the storm, both physically and mentally. Just as in combat, these social exchanges happen in a flash, and you need to be properly trained.

That said, social judo often works, and it can be very empowering for your son. Because constant conflict is so draining I think social judo needs to stand as the main go-to strategy for your son. It will be wonderful if he can turn 'bullies into buddies'. What a win! But also, staying in this bandwidth keeps your son in a positive space regarding his social world. Others will see his friendly, positive disposition and be drawn to him. He will come across as confident in himself and friendly to others, even in difficult circumstances.

So don't hate

As one surprisingly insightful young boy said, hating involves a mixture of anger, fear, stress, and sadness. It will really help your son if he can let this go, and off a base of 'same-as' respect, keep inviting his tormentor into the better way.

Here are some reasons to not hate:

1. **Hating is tiring. Hating is hard work.** It cultivates a negative, aggravating emotion, and it causes physiological stress. Every time you think about a person you hate, your body secretes stress hormones – your body tenses up and you feel angry. So long-term hating can end up damaging us.

2. **You'll end up thinking a lot more about them.** Hatred is linked to danger or threat, and we're wired to stay alert to these things. As a result, we tend to think a lot about people we hate. Especially when we're not busy or preoccupied. This means people who've hurt us can occupy our minds and spoil our actual, real-time lives.

3. **You'll be wrong.** If you hate someone, you'll be engaged in 'splitting', where people are seen as all good or all bad. This dehumanises others, and it also makes us far less creative and thoughtful in our interpersonal dealings. As hard as it may be, your son needs to remember that his tormentors are human beings, with their own strengths and vulnerabilities.

4. **You'll be stuck in patterns of fear.** You will avoid situations where 'they' are. You will also venture less of yourself – in class, on the sports field, and elsewhere. You could even quit things you actually like, making your own world shrink.

5. **Your other relationships will be affected.** Because you are tense and on the defensive, you'll be less light-hearted, less open, more guarded than friendly. Other people will read your body language, and assume you don't want to be approached, or invited to join in.

So help your son look for things he can admire in each of the boys, including his antagonists. I'm not saying you and your son shouldn't reflect on these boys' failings. I think this kind of perspective taking is useful. When I'm working with a boy, we do talk about this. I want a boy to realise his tormentors are human, and that they have their own fears and insecurities.

Still, I don't want him to condemn them as 'less than'. If a boy copes by cultivating a sense of disdain or superiority, he's likely to provoke further antagonism. In any case, this one-up, superior position is fake – brittle. It will actually keep your son tense – on the defensive. I also know that from this negative position, your son won't be able to use the kinds of strategies that work. Instead, he will be stuck in a negative pattern.

Mutual respect

Nevertheless, both 'be a good guy', and social judo are based on respect both for others *and for oneself.* To maintain this line, there will be times your son will need to stand up for himself, be firm, and tell boys just where to get off. In other words, your son will need to know his boundaries.

Boundaries: A sliding scale of assertiveness

Boundaries demarcate a healthy 'inside-outside' dynamic. They are crucial to effective community functioning. I remind boys that boundaries aren't meant to be walls, separating people; they're lines of healthy connection between yourself and others.

To spruce up boys' understanding of boundaries, I like to use the analogy of farming. I say:

Imagine you own a farm. One Sunday, you're relaxing inside, and suddenly you hear hooting. You realise it's coming from your gate. You make your way out there, and you see some guys in a truck, with cows on the back. They shout out at you, saying, 'Open up man, our cattle are hungry! You've got good grass on your farm. We want it!'

You'd say? (if I need to, I help them here).

You'd say 'No way, this is a farm. I need the grass for my own cattle. Anyway, this is private property. And it's a Sunday. You'll need to reverse your truck and leave – sorry'.

What if they don't? What if they carry on hooting? And what if they start cutting the fence?

You'd say? (if I need to, I'll help them here).

Responses vary: *'Give another warning', or 'Call the police', or 'Get my rifle' etc.*

Sometimes, depending on the circumstances the boy is facing, I say:

"And what would you do if some of them circled around your property, found a way in, and actually came into your house? What would you do if one or two of them started to attack you, or someone you love?"

Ok, so this is my way. There are many ways to make the point. But I want boys to understand the concept of a boundary violation, and of a 'sliding scale of assertiveness'. I want them to feel the logic and rightness of it, so they can build this inside themselves.

The scale of assertiveness is likely to go along these lines:

1. Understand the law (what's right)

2. Make a request to desist

3. Repeat the request – clarifying the law.

4. Repeat the request with a warning if the request is ignored (such as "I'm going to call the cops").

5. Calling the cops

6. And if the home is threatened, be able to defend yourself.

7. And if you or your loved ones is attacked, be able to use whatever force is necessary to defend both yourself and them.

Now school communities are actually quite a bit more complicated than this kind of 'one-off' rural incident. Within schools, you live alongside your antagonists. As far as possible, you've got to try and keep good relationships with as many people as you can. And turning to the Law is by no means simple.

Still though, if we think of the farm as being the self, I want a boy to realise he has a right to defend his selfhood, and that he must practice a sliding scale of assertiveness. This mitigates against the two most common problematic responses:

1. Over-reaction (getting too emotional – shouting out or losing self-control)

2. Excessive timidity (being an easy target)

Boys who get too upset, or overly emotional, tend to invite further bullying and put-downs, as do boys who are defenceless or seemingly helpless. You want your son to avoid both extremes, and one way of doing this involves exercising a sliding scale of assertiveness. Within school, the sliding scale needs to include the following dimensions:

1. Be a good guy

2. Social Judo

3. Reverse Mirroring

4. A line in the sand

5. Recognise bullying

6. A message in the meanness?

7. Toughen up

8. Be rough stuff ready

Reverse mirroring

As I say, social Judo doesn't always work. Partly, this is because the skills aren't that easy to apply. But also, bullies can brush past pro-social invitations, and they know how to make a boy feel really bad. Bullies can be very confident, physically strong, emotionally hard, and well-liked. They almost always have crowd backing, and they know how to elicit group laughter, or general derision. A lot of their power comes from this. Put simply, a bully can make a boy feel terrible – the outsider – the weird one – the loser of the group.

I talk with young people about this. I say:

"Part of the reason you feel so bad, and so stressed, is because when he says that, everyone's eyes are on you – like you're being viewed as an object of failure.

Subconsciously, this is what these guys do – they get everyone to look at you – so it feels like everyone's judging you. Bud, I think it's time to reverse the mirror.

We can't let this guy keep acting like this. You've tried to be the better person. You've invited him into better ways. But he's stuck on putting you down. So I think you need to get more assertive. I think it's time to call him out for his ways. Next time he says this to you, I want you to say:

"Shoo, that was pretty harsh"

OR

"Yoo Michael, you can be harsh with your words"

OR

"Yoo Michael – you seem to like putting me down".

OR

'Michael, you can be a real bully sometimes'

OR

'Michael, you're being a bully'

Then I ask a boy to say the phrase back to me. Often I tweak what he says, and how he says it. I don't want the words to be too harsh or too gentle. I want him to know how to call a boy out, but in a non-condemning way. You might notice that my examples go from a relatively benign observation ("that was pretty harsh") to a direct and pretty assertive statement ("you're being a bully"). Yet throughout, I go for phrases that are honest without being aggressive or insulting. This is why, even as I up the ante, I use words like "you can be" and "sometimes", rather than something accusatory like "you're a bully". I'm looking for a truth statement, I'm not looking for a fight.

I also pay attention to things like body language and the tone a boy uses. I want him to be able to say the words in a clear and confident way – like he means what he says. And I want his posture to be right. In social spaces, body language is so important. Help your son to express what he's saying in the right way. Get him to practice with you. You be the antagonist, and let him practice saying what he needs to say with you. Then swap roles. Let him see the impact it can have.

One boy liked the phrase "Shoo, that was pretty harsh!" or sometimes just "Yow, harsh!" He practiced it with me. He practiced saying it with a relaxed body *and a smile.* He wanted to show others that his core self was still strong. But we also anticipated that his main protagonist would mock this statement, by repeating it in a high, sing-song voice. So the boy also practiced shrugging his shoulders, turning up his palms, and signifying "Whatever" with his face – as in 'what you've just done doesn't affect me and is even a bit silly'.

This worked well. Other boys in the group saw how this boy handled the put-down. They noticed his calmness, his friendliness, and his inner strength. And they liked him for it. Of course there are any number of variations of 'what to say, and how to say it'. I don't know what will fit your son's circumstance. Each situation is nuanced, and each school has its own in-house way of saying things. At the end of the day, your son needs to be comfortable with what he says, and ready enough to use it.

The overall goal is to reverse the social mirror, so that for a moment, the group gaze turns towards the attacker, and he's called out for his ways. A mirror statement can also provide a base from which your son can ward off immediate further attacks. What I mean is, if the bully ups the ante, and shoots off another put-down, this only serves as evidence of the truth your son has just identified.

It looks like this:

"No-one likes you"

Son: "Shoo Michael. You can be really harsh with your words"

(Laughter) "Ja well it's the truth"

Son: "Like I say…"

"Ah well, you're a real jerk"

Son: "Like I say..."

Now look, socially speaking, the 'reverse mirror' strategy can be quite a slap. Any boy who's had the mirror reversed on him will likely feel its sting, and remember what was said for a long time to come. You can't use it all the time. It's usually reserved for certain moments, rather than being an everyday thing. But it's very appropriate when the above two strategies (be a good guy and social judo) aren't bearing fruit, and a boy needs to stand his ground – and be more assertive. It also prepares the way for the following strategy.

A line in the sand

If things don't change, your son might need to take a deep breath, and tell whoever's targeting him to stop – or else. This can be a big step for a boy, because it brings things to a head. All the same, sometimes it's called for. Things have gone on too long. For your son's sake, he needs to take a stand – draw a line in the sand and say "No further!"

As I say, this is not easy territory for most boys, and it's likely your son will need your advice. So get into the details of your son's situation. How assertive or direct should he be? Will a friendly, yet still direct talk suffice, or does your son need to be pretty firm about it? Should your son speak to the boy in private, or would it be better if your son had someone to support him during the exchange? Help your son think through all this. There are many possible variations.

For instance, maybe the offending boy and your son are 'sort of friends'. If so, it could be enough for your son to call the boy to one side, and say something like:

"Mark, you're a good guy, but when you ... then it's not cool. Please stop!"

(Note: the "you're a good guy" phrase incorporates both 'Social Judo' and 'Be a good guy' principles.)

Of course, the 'sort of friend' may not listen the first time, so perhaps your son could then say something along the lines of:

"Mark, bud, I've asked you to stop, but I don't know, it's like you aren't hearing me. I'm telling you now I've had enough. If you do it again, then although I don't want to, I'll need to take it further".

However, maybe the offending boy isn't a friend at all. Perhaps he's consistently mean, and something of a bully. This is difficult. It's tough to confront someone more powerful than you, and always, there's the ghastly prospect of being called a snitch.

In the midst of these realities, perhaps it would be better for your son to have friends (or a senior boy, or a teacher) with him as he goes about 'drawing his line'. In terms of what he should say, I'd suggest something like:

"Jason, I've asked you to stop. Many times. No longer. Now you really need to cut it out. Or I'll need to take it further"

As you can see, I like the phrase 'take it further'. I like that it's vague. Keeping it a mystery adds to its impact. Let the offender worry about just what 'taking it further' could mean. Also, keeping things vague keeps options open for your son, and somewhat buffers him from the dreaded tag of being 'a snitch'.

If the offender presses your son about this, your son could reply in the following kind of way:

"Ah well, what are you going to do?"

"You'll see ... "

"Yeah, but what?"

"You'll see"

If your son speaks in the company of others, he could also say something like:

"And you can't complain if it does happen, because now I've warned you"

I suggest this step because it *somewhat* diverts away from the problem of being labelled a snitch. Witnesses have heard your son give the warning, so hopefully the wider group will understand if he does report what's happening to a school authority.

Again, oftentimes, even though the offender knows there could be consequences, he doesn't stop. If this happens, your son should:

- Speak to an older, more senior boy. Perhaps a prefect. Explain what's happening. Ask him to speak to the boy on your behalf

- If the boy still won't listen, turn to the school counsellor or a member of staff. Ask them to give you advice or to take it forward. Where appropriate, school staff may opt to work with the group, or take one or two boys aside, to gain further insights and to give direction regarding what needs to happen next. This can include disciplinary measures.

Turning to teachers

Safe teachers, who know the system, can be very important resources throughout the above process. What do I mean by 'safe'? I mean the teachers who will listen, the teachers your son likes, and the teachers he feels know him best. Safe teachers understand how the school works. They also understand boy dynamics. Safe teachers have good EQ, they get on well with teenagers, and they keep good boundaries. Safe teachers won't overreact, but they also won't underreact, or do nothing.

Encourage your son to turn to these teachers, before things get too bad. With safe teachers, boys can explain their situation and ask their advice. From what I've seen, many boys don't want teachers to directly intervene.

They say something like *"Sir, I don't want you to do or say anything, I just want you to know. This is what I'm thinking of doing. How does it sound?"*

Boys like to use teachers, parents, and other adults as sounding boards, but they often want to be given space to sort the problem out themselves. For the most part, this is good, as you want your son to feel empowered and more equipped to deal with his social problems. Also, interventions 'from above' invariably trample over subtleties in the ecology of the adolescent group, sometimes causing damage rather than restoration.

That's why I recommend a step-wise approach. You want your son to assert himself in healthy ways, and to give his antagonists the opportunity to change their ways. As his parent, you're too far away to successfully intervene. Personally, I've never seen social engineering work – so phoning other parents' kids, or inviting certain 'nice' boys home, or directly confronting boys yourself (it happens) doesn't work. You have to walk in step with your son, keep faith in him, and perhaps garner insights from members of staff who know your son and the other boys. There are, however, definitely times when parents need to step in. This certainly applies to the problem of bullying.

Recognise bullying

Whenever a child gets hurt by peers, the important issue of bullying emerges. And if it's your child, it's urgent. In your alarm, you may feel yes – this is bullying! But then again, you might not be so sure. As one parent put it:

"You know, to us it was like – no way! That's bullying! But I guess it's always like that. When it happens to your child you always feel like 'Ah – that's bullying".

I understand. We're wired to protect our kids. We know our son's vulnerability. We feel his pain. And we're outraged. We want the nonsense to stop, and we want the perpetrators to be properly dealt with by the school – now!

We could be right about the bullying. Yet from what I've seen the matter is often not as straightforward as we'd like it to be. So again, before you press the 'go' button, find out as much as you can about the context. Try to understand the ecology of your son's group. If you charge in, and insist on action, you could easily end up making things worse. As parents, we must take the time to find out more about what's going on.

Take it from me, groups of boys can be very harsh with each other. They can say and do awful – even hurtful things – but within context it's not meant to be destructive. The mean boys could actually be quite nice boys who don't realise the impact of their words and actions. They could consider your son a friend.

Also, your son might be telling only half the story. He could also be involved in the culture of meanness, giving as good as he gets, without you even knowing. If any of this is the case, the label of bullying doesn't quite fit, and invoking severe sanctions could be a mistake. I know it sounds weird, and maybe even wrong. But remember, we're dealing with teenage boys.

Having said all this, there really is such a thing as bullying, and when it happens it's a serious problem. According to Dan Olweus, an expert in the field, a few things set bullying apart:

1. Bullying involves **negative actions** (e.g. taunting, teasing, name calling, hitting, pushing, kicking, restraining, pinching, excluding, sneering, making insulting gestures).
   (Here, I pay particular attention to the presence of cruelty. Bullying is nasty and damaging; it's intended to harm a person's selfhood).

2. Bullying involves a **power imbalance**. Bullies are stronger (physically and/or psychologically) than their victims.

3. Bullying happens **repeatedly** through the course of a school day or week

4. Bullying describes behaviour that's **entrenched** – it's been going on for some time.

Taken together, the above factors depict a child who is helpless – stuck in a very damaging situation that he *can't solve on his own*. Such a child needs adults to intervene on his behalf.

If I thought my son was being bullied, I would:

- Make contact with a senior teacher, and ask for an urgent meeting where I can raise my concerns.

- I'd also ask the teacher if, before we met, he or she could gather in-house information, to clarify the school's take on my son's situation.

- If, during the meeting, it's agreed that my son is being bullied, I'd ask for the situation to be dealt with according to the school's formal protocols.

- This would include any kind of online put-downs, abuse or cyberbullying which, as I say, are always beyond the pale.

- If the question of 'is this bullying or not' remains undecided, I'd ask for ideas and advice regarding how my son can be helped going forward. Who can he turn to? Where? When? Might some kind of group/class intervention be appropriate? Do other boys need to be spoken to? If so, how can my son's well-being and integrity be safeguarded?

- When a boy gets targeted by a powerful member of the group, *other boys tend to either keep quiet or they join in.* So I'd want a strategy that included the roles played by other boys. Other boys, fearful of being targeted themselves, sometimes gain favour by aligning with the bully. The whole group can turn against a boy, shunning and isolating him. This is obviously extremely painful, and it's not something a boy can deal with on his own. He needs a member of staff to intervene. Other boys in the group need to realise what they're doing (because they won't). They need to be challenged and guided on ways that they can support the victim, especially when he's being treated badly. It involves simple but courageous things like sitting next to the boy in class or the dining room, asking him to join in group activities. Some boys may even be willing and able to challenge a bully when he's being mean.

- This is so important. When boys are taught to support others, true masculine strength emerges. Instead of using their power to attack 'difference', boys learn that true masculine strength is displayed by standing alongside the marginalised. Everyone wins when young men learn to deploy their strength for the sake of others rather than for themselves. Boys can do it, but often they need guidance.

I'll never forget, at the very start of the year, making my way towards my desk. And – what the heck – I was sitting next to Steven X – again! My nemesis – a guy who'd tormented me for ages!

Anyway, I sit down, and he starts with his chirps – again. Then Michael, one of the biggest guys in the grade, turns round to Steven, points his finger at him, and says "No more of that". And that was it! That was all it was. Steven left me alone after that.

Now, as I say, your son is likely to worry that intervention will make things worse. He could become alarmed and angry. He could beg you to do nothing. If this was the case I'd talk to my son about the rightness of boundaries, about abuses of power, and the fact that he's entitled to feel safe at his own school.

I'd also run through the various strategies described above, and if my son thinks he's missed a step, I'd say he needs to take it pronto, if I'm to hold off the cavalry. For instance, my son could say he wants to try the 'or else' strategy with the bully (perhaps with one or two friends in tow). I might be ok with this. Perhaps it will work, and my son will end up feeling empowered in the process. But then I'd need observer confirmation and I'd definitely ask a teacher to monitor things going forward.

The truth is, there's often some fallout following an intervention. When a powerful or influential boy gets punished, or perhaps even expelled, the victim can face significant peer criticism, and some boys may remain angry with him for a long time. So there can be a price to pay. Still, for me, these are short-term costs. In the long term, I hope and trust your son will realise why you did what you did – the rightness of it – and how you couldn't just stand by while he was being bullied.

A message in the meanness?

This is a tough one for sure, and maybe even unfair. Your child is hurting. He's in the 'one-down' position – the one without the power. Even so, I think it's worth looking to see if there's a 'message in the meanness'.

What do I mean? Well, teasing isn't always and only about being mean. It's also a common way people try to get someone to change. As a strategy, it's hurtful and ineffective, yet many people still use it. It's certainly common in marriages. We get irritated with our partners. We don't like some of their ways. And so we use snide comments or put-downs, to try to get them to change. Of course, it never works. It simply raises tensions, and puts our partners on the defensive.

Terrence Real, an expert on relationships, describes how we get stuck in 'the more-the more' patterns of relating. In other words, 'the more I … the more you…' This dynamic could apply to your son. Something about him could be irritating or frustrating his peers. They give him negative feedback, which puts his back up, or makes him tense, and without realising it he becomes more (in their eyes) irritating.

Of course this cycle (the more/the more) works both ways, so it's not about putting all of the blame on your son. You could also say that *because* of the way a boy is treated, he loses confidence, becomes tense and upset, and it's very hard for him to be his usual, friendly, best self within the group.

All the same, to get out of the cycle, you and your son need to focus on the things he can control. Bullying expert Dan Olweus talks about 'provocative victims', who may be 'hot tempered', who fight or answer back when they're insulted. They may be overly excitable, over-active, or have irritating habits and immature ways. Personal mannerisms and habits can become a real issue within the close quarters of a boarding school.

Or, your son could be overly passive or submissive. Perhaps carries a lot of self-doubts. Maybe he struggles to assert himself, allowing others to take advantage of him. Maybe your son is anxious about his physical self. He may not like the way he looks, or he may feel weak and uncoordinated, which puts him on the back foot when it comes to sport or rough and tumble spaces.

As a parent, you might be able to guess at the reason behind the teasing, but you don't want to raise it. You don't want to hurt your son even more. You'd rather build him up. I think this is why parents say stuff like "don't worry, they're just jealous". The thing is, it's hardly ever true, and your son knows it.

As I've said, boys agonise over the question "Why me?", and I think they need a real answer. With a real answer in place, a boy can work towards making some healthy responses. But if he stays unsure, and his faults remain cloaked, he will be stuck. He will also be at risk of *excessive self-criticism – drawing conclusions that are far worse than the truth.* Remember, clear bad news is invariably better than uncertainty. Clarity, even if it hurts a bit, paves the way for new action and growth.

Yet how do we go about this? How do we steer our sons towards more effective behaviours, without hurting them in the process. It's tricky. One careless word from us could devastate our sons.

True self, social self, and false self

My approach is to separate the 'true self' from the 'social self'. To me, the 'true self' refers to a person's core nature. You know your son. You know he came to you with a certain temperament, and with particular likes and dislikes. It's just the way he is. Whenever I recognise this in a person, I feel like I'm encountering something sacred, something about his personhood, that I *should not try to change*.

I think you know what I mean. You meet with a person, and you get a sense of his or her unique presence. This presence includes aspects like temperament, personality, innate talents and strengths, and social style. I see these features in the way a boy acts with me, and through the stories he tells. It's not that difficult, to be honest.

The social self refers to the person we *learn* to present to the world. It's a way of being, that works 'out there'. All good parents help their children to develop this self. It happens spontaneously within the home, through the every-day values of the family microcosm. For example, you might expect your child to do certain chores, or to pick up after himself, or to greet visitors, and to say sorry when he messes up. These are values you uphold, and you want to instil them in your child. It's not about developing a 'false self', it's about becoming socially capable.

All of the strategies described in this book are aimed at developing your son's social self. They are not about changing his core self. In fact, I want your son to accept and celebrate who he is, while at the same time realising that he can grow.

I think this mitigates against damage. If your son has been born with a sensitive temperament, you want him to accept and celebrate that. Similarly, if he's an introvert, then great! Perhaps he could read Susan Cain's book *Quiet* to get a sense of the many strengths that come with this. If your son has some form of ADHD, perhaps you could point him to Thom Hartmann's novel perspective on the abilities inherent in ADHD. I often encourage boys to read stories about adults with ADHD, to see how they've found success through a combination of awareness, acceptance, and social strategy. There are many such stories, and they invariably describe a combination of 'true self' acceptance and 'social self' growth.

So as I get to know a boy, I get a sense of who he is, as well as the things I think he needs to change. When it comes to aspects he can't or shouldn't try to change (his true self), I *always* cast them in the positive – as inherent qualities. However, I also need to guide the boy's social self, because he isn't acting in optimal ways, and this needs to be addressed.

So my advice is invariably along the lines of: "I really appreciate ... about you, but be careful of/ perhaps think about .... "

It looks like this:

I so appreciate your kind nature, but don't let yourself be taken for a ride

Shoo Nick, you have a quick grasp of right and wrong. But with some of these guys, it's probably not worth pointing anything out. What do you think?

I like how you weigh things up. There's a lot of wisdom in that. But sometimes it might be better to just press the 'go' button, and give yourself a chance?

You seem to have a natural ability to take charge. That's really great. Leadership takes a lot of practice though. I guess it's just so easy for people to just see it as being bossy?

You really are willing to look at yourself. But gosh, watch that you don't become overly self-critical. I hope you can also see all your good qualities

Bud, I get that you find people draining. I can relate! Just watch that you don't give people the idea that you don't like them though.

Shoo bud, you have a Ferrari engine in there (pointing to his chest). Such great energy! Just don't want you to keep getting pinged for it though. Perhaps we can look at ways you can drop the revs when you're in class?

I hope these examples give you enough of an idea. There's so much about our children that needs to be accepted, respected, and loved. At the same time, your son is not the finished product. So it's about acceptance and guidance.

It's a two-step process. Acceptance is the base for growth and change. If your son is emotionally intense, then so be it. Show him how to manage himself from that truth. If he gets anxious, and he battles to stand up for himself, show him how to make choices in the midst of his fear, rather than to pretend it isn't there.

Without this kind of guidance, boys won't know what to do with their vulnerabilities. They may deny, come to hate, or feel very defensive about aspects of themselves. Boys are especially at risk of suppressing their emotional selves for the sake of peer approval. All this can lead to restricted, brittle, 'false self' development, and the risk of significant fallout further down the road.

Self-other respect

This two-step process focuses on relational values, or me-you respect. It's nourishing rather than damaging. Children don't mind when we ask them to behave in pro-social ways. They know that good values matter. So I want you to expect your son to respect others. But I also want you to teach your son to walk tall, and to draw a line if others treat him with disrespect.

Again though, all this needs to be founded on self-awareness and self-acceptance. This is where children can be hurt – when we dismiss or discredit their inner experiences, in our efforts to change who they are.

Off the base of self-awareness and acceptance, your son can be equipped to say things like:

"Look, I know I can be quite loud, but that doesn't mean you can talk to me like that."

OR

"Sorry man, it's just that I need down time every now and again. Ok to play Squash tomorrow instead?"

A boy who can speak like this holds his selfhood in a very healthy way. He's self-aware, he accepts who he is, including his foibles. This combination of self-acceptance and ongoing growth protects his dignity and promotes a sense of optimism about the future. Other boys will see and respond to his combination of self-awareness, humility, and inner strength.

Touchy Topics?

What if there's no message – no grain of truth in the meanness? What if boys are simply being mean, targeting highly sensitive aspects such as your son's appearance, or his sporting, or academic ability? My approach is somewhat similar. It includes the following three steps:

1. Acknowledge the pain (of feeling physically inadequate/not sporty/ clever enough).

2. Recognise your son's inherent strengths in the midst of his pain. For instance, over the years I've worked with many boys who struggle at school due to specific learning difficulties. I've seen boys become increasingly despondent about this, and by Grade 10 or so, many of them are close to giving up. Yet once they start to talk about the truth of their pain and frustration, I get a chance to highlight their inherent strengths. I say things like *"Wow bud, it's been really hard for you. How the heck have you managed to hang in for so long? Where do you find the courage?"*

3. Steps 1 and 2 give you a platform to guide your son in the world out there. Again, if I meet with a boy who's struggling academically, I talk about strategies he can use, not only to persevere, but to persevere in

better, healthier ways. Many boys give up on their own intelligence. They believe they aren't clever, and so they stop thinking. As soon as work hits the desk, their brains shut down. So I try to get them to think about intelligence in new ways. We discuss concepts like Carol Dweck's 'growth mindset', which points to the transformative effects of persevering through difficulty. I also look to buffer a boy against anxiety and despair, and to explore learning strategies that will best suit who he is as a person.

The thing is, I never want a boy to give up on himself. I've walked alongside a lot of young people and, time and again, I've seen how much they can change. As I write this I think of a young adolescent who was being teased for being overweight, and for being 'useless' at sport. If I didn't know what I know, I might have said something like:

"Bud, never mind, maybe sport just isn't your thing. Perhaps you should find something you can be good at – something that suits you more?"

Yet if I'd said that to his fourteen year-old self, I'd have been dead wrong. Fact is, he loved a particular sport (a sign of his true self), and the more he played, the better he got. And by the time he was eighteen he was a lean and muscular monster! I sometimes think *"What if I had told him to pack up his sport aspirations?"* Had I done that, I might have stolen possibility from him. I might have cursed his unfolding.

Again, these three steps make it possible for your son to accept and respect who he is, without losing hope in his capacity to grow. With this base in place, boys who carry perceived deficiencies can say things like:

"It's true. This Maths is giving me a real headache! Ah well, round two tomorrow. I guess we all have to walk our own roads, hey?"

Size, shape, and ability. This then, is how I help a boy to cope, when such personal attributes are targeted.

Toughen up

I don't mean to be a jerk. But if you're in a group of adolescent boys, who are caught up in the humour involved in put-downs, you need to learn to take it. A big part of this is learning to not take it personally. Another big part is seeing this space as an opportunity to become tougher.

In some male spaces, this ability is required. Adopting a certain rough attitude to the self is part of earning membership – being one of the boys. We might think it's wrong – that boys shouldn't be so mean to each other. But it is what it is. And it's definitely present in certain adult contexts.

Let me give you an example: A while ago my son wanted to join an anti-poaching unit, who work to protect targeted wildlife in our many beautiful reserves. This meant he had to go through a very demanding, military-like basic training. It was a physical challenge for sure. But more than that, it was an emotional challenge. You were treated like dirt. You were yelled at. Crude and demeaning things were said about you. No one cared how you felt. You had to endure. That's it.

Now my son had to face this. He couldn't take it personally. He had to realise it was part of the context. This is how it was. You have to have a thick skin. You have to roll with the punches and take up the kind of dark humour that comes from shared hardship. Understandably, at the end of it all, my son was very proud. And he'd also made some good friends along the way. I realise this book focuses on young people, not men. But I want to show that there's a certain utility in helping our sons know how to take teasing without falling apart.

To achieve this kind of toughness, you have to change your attitude. You have to remember it's about the context, not you. It's about the culture of the place, and who one has to be in order to prevail.

In boarding school contexts, many boy problems centre around being too much. What do I mean? Well, in boy culture, you don't want to be the guy who's too emotional, too loud, too active, too excitable, or trying too hard (to be funny, clever, or popular). You gotta know how to play it cool. You gotta know how to laugh at yourself. And you gotta be able to roll with the punches.

This is why many boys learn to mute the self for a while. Especially in group settings. Even this simple step can be helpful for a season. I do want your son to do much more than survive school. But for a while, he may need to learn how to cope before he can thrive. He needs to develop a 'boarding school self' – a self that can laugh at put-downs because he understands the context.

A while back I met with a youngster who'd come through a difficult first year, and then prevailed. I asked him how he did it – and what he'd learned. He said:

"I realised they actually want a reaction. So if I got upset, went and lay on my bed, or got angry, and tried to fight back – it just got worse. So now I've learned how to play along with the joke. Or if I just put a smile on my face, they'll leave me alone. So I think I've learned not to take it so seriously.

Ah, I just think I was immature actually. Sometimes I tried to be funny, but I was just silly, and they don't take that well".

Toxic masculinity?
We have to be careful. The toughness involved in peer banter can certainly slide into peer abuse – where anyone who's different is demeaned, harassed, and tormented. But this indicates boys who are misguided – boys who think toughness is about meanness, and not caring for anything, except one's reputation.

This is a brittle kind of masculinity, and I've no interest in it. It's a masculinity that's going nowhere, because it's actually just posturing, and it has nothing meaningful to offer the world.

So your son needs to remember what's good, and to stand for that. In the rough and tumble of social life, he needs to become strong enough to tolerate put-downs without falling apart, and clear minded enough to draw the line should teasing cross into disrespect. Healthy masculinity is not about disrespect. In fact, in healthy male groups, there is kindness. It's just covert. It's about laughing at your jokes, saving you a seat, inviting you to the party, hearing your ideas, and recognising your abilities. In girl groups, you lead with kindness. In boy groups, you lead with toughness. But kindness follows. And it can be surprisingly tender.

Take my son Matt. After one particularly gruelling day, his Sergeant pulled up alongside the group, and asked if any of them had blisters. Silence. The guys were suspicious. Maybe this was this some kind of trick – a perverse way of springing yet another hard PT session. Seeing their hesitancy, the sergeant asked again "Who's got blisters?" After a few moments, everyone in the group raised their hands. And one by one, he called them up to the back of the truck, took off their shoes, cleaned their feet, and applied antiseptic ointment. My son calls it a Jesus moment. The group bonded all the more, and the sergeant was held in even higher regard.

Toxic masculinity is founded on fake toughness – on apparently 'not caring' about anyone or anything, including yourself. What I'm looking for is not machismo, or the glorification of power and aggression. I'm looking for a less flashy, less intoxicating, but surer strength. The ability to stand for what is good. The ability to accept and even smile at one's failings. The ability to tolerate jibes and even criticisms without falling apart. And the ability to move towards creative action and expression in the midst of all of this. I'm looking for the ability to stay a 'good guy', to grow, to get better, even in the midst of meanness. Almost all boys will respond positively to this kind of strength, even if they take a bit of time to see it in your son.

Be rough stuff ready

Look, my son's a timid, gentle guy. He's just never been one to enjoy roughhousing at school. He'd rather just step back, and hang around the quieter, nicer guys. Anyway, around grade eight a couple of boys started picking on him – making his life miserable at break and during sports practices. And he was falling apart. So we asked him if he'd like to take up Karate, and he was pretty keen, actually. He ended up really loving the sessions. I'll always remember at his first lesson – his head thrown back – yelling out 'KI YA!' as he threw out punches in time with the Sensei.

I don't know, it was like he really needed that – to feel empowered maybe – for the first time in ages. .

I think it's good for a boy to know how to defend himself, if things get physical. Being a good guy is important, but it's better to act from a position of strength, rather than weakness. If your son lacks confidence in his physical self, and he can't defend himself, he's more likely to be passive, and overly wary of physically assertive boys. Unfortunately this can make him an easy target for bullies.

So if you're able, show your son how he can defend himself if someone tries to shove, hit, or pin him down. If you don't know, call on someone who does. It's not that I want your son to get involved in fights, or become someone he's not. It's that I want him to know he can defend himself if needed. If your son can protect himself physically, it will be easier for him to assert healthy boundaries in the rough and tumble of boy life.

Not just backing down

Invariably, this coincides with a change of attitude. As a boy gets stronger, and more able to defend himself, he grows in confidence. He develops the ability to meet and – if needs be – match, other boys' aggression. As one student put it:

I tried being gentle, not being rough, but now it's like, if they're not going to listen, I'll just have to be rough. So now, if they bump into me or pull my bag something, I turn around and just say 'piss off'. And it's working – they leave me alone now.

Reflecting further, he said:

I don't know, I guess I was just scared of being physical – like I didn't want to be a trouble-maker or something.

To which I replied:

Yet it turns out you're becoming more of a trouble-ender nowadays

The thing is, with boys, physical strength matters. Your son could feel happier in himself if he starts to feel that he's getting stronger. He may not like physical exercise, especially in the presence of other boys. Yet at the same time, your son might feel insecure about his physical appearance, and wish he had some muscles or a flatter stomach. So he could be open to more private ways of exercising – perhaps a few weights, resistance bands, or some kind of online instruction.

Of course, exercise also helps hugely with stress and mood management, and many boys notice how they feel better after their workout session. For many, it's the gym, and I'm always happy when they go with friends. For others, especially if they're carrying a lot of stress, rhythmical exercises like swimming, or cycling, or running, or rowing machines are best.

Find your voice

I said earlier that it can be effective for your son to mute himself for a season. But we have to watch this. It can easily become a long-term normal, where your son takes up an invisible life in order to minimise peer put-downs. From this place, your son won't be able to perform at his creative best. He's always afraid.

I think of a young man I met some time ago. He'd been an excellent sportsman at junior school. But in his first year of high school, through no fault of his own, he fell foul of his peer group. As a result, he suffered a lot of meanness, and this derailed him. He couldn't express himself properly. Out there on the sports field, in the midst of his peers, he couldn't feel free. He couldn't tap into his talent. He couldn't 'just play'. Instead, he was tense, stressed, and clumsy. Unfortunately this peer problem never came out in the open. So he never addressed it. Instead, he tried to live with it, and he left school without ever doing justice to his abilities.

If someone had known, they could have helped him step out of his shame state, and recover a healthier sense of self. He could have come to a better sense of his peer group, who the good guys were, and the trap of mind reading. He could have broken out of the vicious cycle, and practiced every day ways of being braver.

Sure, perhaps he'd need to tolerate standing on his own for a season. But he could do that from a position of strength, not of shame. He could have been helped to reclaim his true self, and to express his gifts, and what he stood for. Then he could have practiced every day ways of living from this position. He could have dusted himself off, reset his goals, and started to really live again. Suddenly, simple concrete actions – like answering a question in class – and practicing hard on the sports field – would have become statements of courage and identity.

Finding meaning

It can be helpful for a boy to find creative ways of expressing all he's been through, and where he's 'at' right now. It could be through writing or journaling, or poetry, or learning to play a musical instrument, or joining a school club or society that chimes with his values. This helps a boy find his voice. It's not just about finding the courage to participate again. It's also about finding space to reflect, to think, and to speak for oneself. This helps a boy to make something good out of his pain.

Find your group

While there's strength in being able to stand alone, it's not a long-term solution. Your son needs to find his group – people who accept and like him. Good friends can offset meanness from other boys. In group spaces, good friends offer solace and security. And for many boys, turning to friends is a key strategy for evading negative interactions.

However, sometimes boys tell me they don't have someone they can turn to, which really worries me. Some isolated boys may turn to the internet to find a sense of belonging. They tell me about friends they've made (but never met), who live in different parts of the world. For me, all this is new, and I don't like to be too quick to dismiss it. In some cases it seems to work, but I think there are distinct risks. Vulnerable, hurting boys can unwittingly give loyalty and allegiance to unsavoury people and groups, and end up being led badly astray.

So, if at all possible, I look for ways a boy can build bonds within his school. As I get a sense of a boy, I like to highlight who he is, and the kinds of social spaces I think he could enjoy. Invariably, I identify one to three social skills that I want a boy to practice, and then I encourage him to step towards other boys with whom I think he can click. Many struggling boys need this, because they're stuck in survival mode and can't see the possibilities around them.

I've also seen how valuable peer communities outside of school can be. And it's a real bonus if that community includes girls. Many boys tell me they can talk more openly with girls, and of course there's nothing like romance to turbo boost one's confidence! The kinds of communities I have in mind include choirs, debating teams, First Aid, and religious-based initiatives. Joining one of these inter-school groups can foster the sense of belonging that boys so desperately need. Having outside friend groups also lessens the impact of internal group meanness, because a boy knows he actually has friends – people who like him. And he knows his peer difficulties are context-based rather than universal.

Get good at something

You know I want your son to be a good guy, but I also want him to enjoy the feeling of getting good at something. He will be so much stronger in himself if he's busy getting good at something challenging; requiring effort, focus, patience, and determination. Such activity can feed your son's sense of self, and positively influence how he's seen by his peers. Also, becoming competent makes it easier for your son to participate, to perhaps join a group or team, making friends along the way.

So whenever I work with a young person, I look out for the things he's naturally drawn to – those interests and activities he just takes to. I also pay attention to who he is as a person, the way he thinks and the way 'life moves him'. I encourage him to see these as emerging strengths, and to take them seriously. I tell him not to worry if other boys seem so much better than him already. I tell him to take a breath, be brave, face forward, and get better in his own right.

The things is, I don't know how a boy is supposed to feel positive about himself when he can't identify something he's either good at, or getting better at. No amount of parental praise or encouragement can substitute for this.

Chapter 5

When to (really) worry?

For me, parenting brought on a whole host of new worries. So, it hasn't been so much when to worry, because I kind of always do. It's standard. Rather, my challenge has been to discern what I should worry about, how much I should worry, and what I should do with my worries.

I imagine you can relate, especially if your son has been struggling with peer difficulties. Yet there is a time when we should *really* worry, because, no doubt about it, meanness can lead to real problems for our sons. Peer meanness can lead to significant mental health difficulties, including anxiety and mood disorders, self-harm, and even the risk of suicide – which is surely every parent's worst nightmare.

So, even as you look to help your son, it's important to acknowledge the risk. Peer difficulties can make a young person feel overwhelmed, lost, and disoriented. Boys can feel and act in ways that are totally out of line with their normal natures, to the point where they can't really hear what we're saying, or use any of our advice. In such cases, proper assessment and help is may well be required.

Here are some of the signs to look out for, if you're worried that your son might be experiencing mental health difficulties:

- Dark, concerning emotions that don't lift after a couple of days?

- Very anxious and agitated, and he can't settle?

- Often sad, tearful, down, or depressed?

- Seemingly angry all the time?

- Sleeping a lot, or hardly at all?

- Stopped doing the things he usually likes to do?

- Started to listen to very sad or 'dark' music?

- Isolating himself?

- Says things like "I hate myself", or "I don't want to live anymore"?

- Any substance abuse, or addictive behaviour?

If you've answered 'yes' to any of these, you need to be more insistent about getting insight into just where your son is at on the inside.

Find the right time to say something like:

Sorry bud, but I'm worried about you. You just haven't been yourself lately. To me, you seem pretty down/sad/stressed/worried. Please help me understand. How are you going on the inside? What's going on?

These are the kinds of questions I ask:

- What is it like for you at school?

- Do you find you're stressed, or tense all the time?

- When do you mostly feel that way?

- Are you feeling down, or not your usual self?

- From - 100 (very down) to + 100 (very happy), where's your mood at the moment? And over the past month?

- Are you feeling lonely, or like you don't have any real friends at the moment?

- Do you sometimes feel empty inside?

- Are you 'in your head' a lot at the moment? Are you 'overthinking things'?

- Are you criticising yourself a lot at the moment, or more than usual?
- Are you battling to sleep at night, or do you just feel like sleeping all the time?
- What goes through your mind at night?

Questions about self-harm

This can be really scary and upsetting territory for parents. None of us wants to believe our child could ever think of harming himself, let alone the terrifying thought that our child might think about taking his own life. So we almost don't want to go there. But if your son is battling, you must be brave, and go there.

You don't have to use fancy words. But do ask the difficult questions. Ask something like:

Bud, does it ever get to the point where you hurt yourself – like punching a wall or cutting yourself?

Do you ever feel like hurting yourself?

Do you ever get a 'what's the point' feeling, where you don't want to live anymore?

Do you sometimes think of taking your life – that it will be easier and better if you were dead?

Have you ever thought of taking your life?

Have you ever made a plan to take your life?

If the answer is 'yes' to any of the above, you must ask:

"Have you tried to take your life?"

Asking your son these questions isn't going to 'put the idea into his head'. If your son isn't feeling suicidal, he's not going to start feeling that way just because you've asked him about it. But it can be a huge relief for a struggling child to finally open up about distressing thoughts and feelings like these. Also, asking these kinds of questions lets you know whether you need to step in, contact the school, and seek professional help. And if your son is struggling in any of these ways, then I really recommend that he sees a professional, so he can be properly assessed and treated.

Is it time to change schools?

It can be very difficult for parents to know whether or not they should take their struggling sons out of boarding. Usually, the dilemma revolves around some key questions: Will it get better? Will my son eventually make friends, and actually start to enjoy himself? If he leaves, will he come to regret leaving this school, with all the opportunities it provides? As loving parents, should we continue to support and push our son towards staying, or is it time to call it quits, and find a different kind of school?

Questions like these can keep a parent up at night. You know your son isn't happy, he says he wants to leave. So now what? What does good parenting look like in this space? Do you tell him to grit his teeth and press on, or do you start talking with the school about an exit strategy?

It's tough to know. Often, things do get better. Many boys do indeed prevail. After a tough period, many boys do turn the corner, start to feel like they belong, and come to really love their school. It doesn't always happen though. Some boys never settle. Some boys never get a sense of belonging and acceptance. Sometimes change is required for a boy to properly thrive.

Yet the very idea of change can be stressful and upsetting. Enrolling at a good school comes with lots of excitement, hopes and dreams – for both the boy and his parents. It's sad to think these hopes and dreams won't be fulfilled. At the end of the day though, we want to do right by our child.

So what are some of the signs that things probably won't work out for the best; that our son actually needs to go to another, and different kind of school?

These are some of the things I look out for:

1. Your son is adamant about leaving

Leaving a school is a big deal for a boy. Often, unhappy boys talk about leaving, but many are just thinking about it – testing the taste of it in their mouths. Also, some boys talk about leaving as a way of indicating how angry and stuck they feel. It's about feelings rather than actual choices. Boys often know that leaving isn't easy – and no straightforward solution for them. The thought of leaving and starting at a new school can cause anxiety for boys. And I've seen how some boys are surprised and rather alarmed when their parents take their 'leave talk' too seriously.

If a boy talks a lot about leaving, I often ask *'percentage wise, how much of you wants to leave, how much of you wants to stay?'* This takes me closer to their actual experience – the bad as well as the good in their world. I also get a sense of just how stuck or hopeless they feel. It paves the way for us to think and talk through the pros and cons of their stay/go choices.

Yet some boys are adamant. They're completely closed to the option of staying. They have no interest in 'in-house solutions'. Their school is 100% bad. And they want out, the sooner the better.

I won't say this is a final nail for me. But my heart does sink. I know that things are going to be hard for this boy: that if he's to stay, his parents will have to endure a long stretch of being 'the bad guys', the ones who 'don't understand'.

2. He never actually wanted to go to boarding school

When a boy is battling, I often ask him why he came to the school in the first place. Did he want to board, or was he forced into it? If a boy came of his own volition, then I know I have some intrinsic impetus to work with – that he came carrying hopes and dreams – an imagined boarding school self. But if a boy doesn't have this, and he's leaned away from boarding from the start, it's going to be very difficult for him to dig in when things get hard. Emotionally and psychologically, he will be set against finding a solution, and set against adults who want him to stay. He will say things like 'my parents don't listen to me' and 'I told them I didn't want to be here'.

Sometimes, as a way of easing a reluctant boy into boarding, parents say something like:

Well just try it. If you don't like it, we'll take you out

Be careful. Again, it will place your son 'on the fence' as a boarder – never really in – and always on the lookout for the horrible. If a boy has this attitude, he will – almost without doubt – see the bad and really battle to see the good. Then you'll be pressed into 'keeping your promise' – perhaps even after his first night!

To get through the difficulties and to properly enjoy and flourish, your son will need intrinsic, authentic 'me' reasons for being at his school. It's so much better if he starts his journey with this in place.

3. The peer problem has persisted for more than 18 months

We mustn't forget how young Grade 8 students are, and what a whirlwind their first year can be. Everything is new, strange, and stressful. Everyone is working out where they fit in, and they're all under pressure and pretty stressed. Even Grade 9 is quite a messy year. The boys are still relatively young, and thoroughly adolescent. Many experienced high school teachers point to Grade 9 as the year when boys are most likely to bring out their ugly.

With this in mind, it's usually worth taking a fair amount of time before concluding that a boy can't make good friends at his school. It's also fair to say that it can take quite a bit of time before boys are practiced enough, *and mature enough*, to properly use the strategies I've described.

Along the way, boys can easily get discouraged. They feel like nothing will work, or things won't change. To this I sometimes say *"The strategies do work, but you may need to grow a bit, and practice a lot, before they do"*.

All the same, it's unfair to expect a boy to keep on trying in the face of impervious negativity and unkindness. And by around midway through Grade 9, adults and educators can start to properly assess the shape of things between the boy and his peer group. If there isn't a compelling way forward, then perhaps it really is time to pull the plug.

4. Your child doesn't have 'bulwark friends' at school

When a boy is struggling with his peers, I always ask (with fingers crossed) if he has at least one or two guys he can count on. Peer meanness is so much worse if you feel like you don't have any friends at all – no-one you can turn to for companionship, laughter, and support.

Obviously a key early strategy is to help a boy build these connections. But often, having no friends at all, is a sign of more complex, intractable problems – either within the child or his circumstances. The problem, of course, is that boarding school is very social. If you live alongside your peers, you need some capacity to form good connections. Five years of high school is too long for anyone to fly solo, and against the flow.

5. Your son doesn't have a sense of belonging

As I say, it can take time for a boy to settle in and 'own' his new school. Still, you can't wait too long. Ultimately, your son needs to feel like he belongs. If your son has been at school for well over a year, and he still feels 'out', something needs to change. Perhaps, in tandem with key teachers, you could allocate one school term for some specific interventions. You'd aim to help your son build better social connections and to help him find meaning in some school activities and pursuits. Is it possible, with social skills training, for him to make better friends? Is it possible for him to set and pursue some personal goals in a school-based activity? Can your son nourish his sense of self and belonging by investing in some aspect of the school programme?

As I write this, I can think of many struggling, 'different' boys who found their place, and became happier, by throwing themselves into some aspect of school life. I can think of boys who've invested in a particular sport, or their academics, or art, music, photography, drama, choir, and outdoor pursuits.

It's not just about being busy, though. Your son still needs friends. Being busy, or even doing well, doesn't equal belonging and acceptance. You can be busy, and even successful, without being liked. Sometimes, a boy puts too much emphasis on what he does. His activity becomes overly important as a marker of self-worth, as in; "in this community, I only matter because I ..." Doing can facilitate, but not solve the problem of belonging. Relational ties still need to be formed.

6. Your child can't perform to his potential or to previous levels

It's a cascading thing. Your son doesn't feel like he belongs, his sense of self is fragmented, and so (obviously) he can't think straight in the classroom, and he can't move properly on the sports field. When you don't fit in, and you feel like you're constantly being put-down, your creativity and coordination go out the window. Innate, natural abilities are choked by anxiety and tension.

Even elite sportsmen are affected. They're brimful with talent. But if they feel like their team mates or coaches don't believe in them, or don't want them there, they won't perform at their best. You see it all the time. Different coaches and different clubs bring different levels of performance from the same players. It's not just better team strategy. It's that the relationships are healthier.

Again, if this is happening, you don't want to overreact as a parent. Lots of boys need to be taught how to perform under pressure, and to cope in competitive 'put-down' spaces, and this takes time. But, for sure, it's worth it. If your son can get stronger in these spaces he will be empowered for years to come. Prevailing against adversity, and coming through under pressure, can be vital ingredients for your son's later successes.

The problem is that relationships are so powerful. How we are seen, how we are treated, can so easily become our truth. And your son is still young. So weigh it up. Is fighting against the social grain worth it for your son? And can he prevail? Time will tell of course, but I wouldn't let too much of high school pass before I made a call on this.

7. Your son actively distances himself from his school.

Some boys, realising they don't fit in, shut up shop and won't (or can't) budge. They're totally closed to "making it work". They 'disidentify' from the school. Deep in their hearts, school becomes the enemy – a 'not me' space.

Signs that your son is in this place are:

- He is not interested or invested in any school activities. He goes through the motions, doing only what he's compelled to do

- He cultivates interests that have nothing to do with the school

- He's always in trouble, and he doesn't seem to care

- You notice that he's destroyed, burnt, or disfigured some items related to school (e.g. school book, tie, or photograph)

- During the holidays, he seldom, if ever, spontaneously tells stories about school. In fact he doesn't like talking about school.

- He's often told you he wants to go to another school

If a boy is stuck in this way of being, it could be time for him to find a different school. Sometimes the boy and the school just don't match. The young person shuts down, or misbehaves, because he can't see a way forward. And sometimes, within that school, and for that child, there isn't one. It really is true that all schools have their own culture, and no single school can fit every child.

Again, due mainly to immaturity, lots of boys are a bit directionless and underinvested at first. And, with guidance, lots of boys do recover, and find better ways of being as they get a bit older. But it's the anti-school self that worries me.

What I'd do, is to think about my son – who he really is – perhaps who he was before this season of his life. And I'd wonder – *if this school was a person, would he and my son be friends? As I contemplate my son's true self, can I picture a slightly older version of him being genuinely happy at this school? Or is there another school that looks like it could be a better, kinder, truer, and more enabling friend to him?*

8. **Your child is battling with mental health difficulties such as anxiety or depression – AND he doesn't want to stay at the school**

Unfortunately, many teenage boys experience mental health difficulties. In these cases, boys need proper treatment, but they don't necessarily need to leave the school. I've worked with many boys who are clinically anxious or depressed, but the thing is, they have friends, they identify with their schools, and they feel like they belong. So when you ask them about leaving, they become alarmed. They say *"No ways. Please no! I don't want to leave. I like it here"*.

For these boys, it's certainly possible to make boarding school work. Obviously, allowances need to be made. Careful assessment and management is required. But it can work. Often, a boy is actually helped by being at school – the structure and busyness of the place, and the friends he has there.

All of this changes, of course, if a boy doesn't have good friends at school, and he faces a lot of peer meanness. In this case, his mental health difficulties are fed and exacerbated by the social difficulties he's experiencing at school.

Calling time

These then, are the kinds of factors I hold in my mind when I meet with a boy who's struggling socially, in the context of boarding. Each factor is important for well-being, and needs to be taken seriously. On its own, each factor makes me worry that "things may not work". However, if a boy presents with a cluster of these factors, then for me, a change may well be required.

It looks something like this: I meet a boy who is constantly being picked on, he has no bulwark friends, he hates boarding, and he's battling with depression. No man. Poor guy! For his sake, he surely needs to move to a different, more suitable school environment.

Thriving

In wrapping up this chapter, let me say that the vast majority of boys do settle into boarding, do end up making good friends, and do end up identifying with their schools. I've been working within boarding schools for over twenty years, and to be honest, I can only think of a handful of boys who couldn't find their way through early social difficulties. Even then, when they've left, a small part of me wishes that they'd stayed.

For the majority of boys, the issue is not about staying or going, it's about making the most of the dynamic, rich, and sometimes challenging social space called Boarding School. You want your son to thrive, not just survive. You want him to learn about himself and others; to make good friends and to leave with good memories, which is what the next chapter is all about.

Chapter 6

And then what happened?

"If you want to know me, then you must know my story, for my story defines who I am"
(Dan McAdams: The stories we live by)

What story are you telling?

When I work with a boy who's struggling, one of my *main aims* is to help him live out a better story. That's what the above strategies are really about. Each strategy requires courage. Each strategy asks a boy to take stock, in the midst of upset and fear, and make a choice towards a more empowered version of himself. To get this point across, I usually say something like this:

Every day you're making choices. And these choices become the story you're telling about yourself and your life. One day, you'll look back at this time. One day, you'll remember feeling stuck and unhappy – just like this. But as an older you, what story do you want to be able to tell? Well, this depends on the choices you make from here, including the choices you make today.

The thing is, I know it's true. I've seen how the high school years live on inside a man – how they weave into his future self – the way he loves, the way he works, and the way he plays.

So the stakes are high. When I meet with a boy, I imagine an older version of himself, and I wonder how he will look back on this time. With this in mind, I try to move a boy along paths where I think he will be able to look back with pride. Not necessarily because of achievements or awards, or even because 'things worked', but because of how he responded to a tough time.

It's a challenge for sure. Yet I feel like I owe it to him. For the sake of his future self, he and I have to find the doors that open out towards good stories. It's hardly ever easy for a boy to go through these doors, but that's kind of the point. I want him to experience the freedom that comes from pressing in, setting the self, and responding creatively in the midst of difficulty.

Of course, he needs to do the walking. I can't do it for him. But he does need help. He needs an adult to help him think through and face his challenges. He needs an adult to help him process tough and hurtful experiences, and to make brave choices when they hit.

Lasting impact

This kind of on-site mentoring is so important. It has a lasting impact. Every so often, I meet up with a high school friend. Invariably, our conversations turn to our high school years. And almost every time we go there, he mentions the time one of his sports coaches called him 'tough'. This potent, one-word endorsement has had such an influence on him. It's settled deep inside of him, serving as an inner resource through all his post-school years.

In that moment, my friend managed to stand strong in the face of an intimidating situation. His team was taking a pounding. The opposition were big and aggressive. His team was demoralised. Yet my friend got stuck in. He didn't give up. He gave as good as he got. On its own, this was an achievement. But it was the coach's affirmation that made the moment bite so deep. It became memorable.

It can be like this for your son. As he starts to gather himself and make the first small steps towards a better story, your recognition and support will make all the difference. You understand how difficult his situation is, because your son has been able to talk with you. And you appreciate his pain, because you've been able to listen. So you can genuinely appreciate the courage he is showing. Every time he's a good guy, you celebrate with him. These moments will become part of the story you share with your son. In time, when the two of you look back, there may be a twist of heartache, but there will also be pride.

The thing is, it's how a story ends that matters. Your son may be struggling. He may be just about at his wits' end. Still, I want you to join him in this place, and help him move towards a good ending. It's not about 'being positive', and it's not about trying to minimise his distress. It's about looking squarely at the reality of his situation, and helping him move forward as creatively as possible.

I believe that by practicing the above strategies, your son can go into his day, ready to tell a better story about himself. When he calls you, he can tell you what he did, rather than what he didn't do. Despite geographical distance, you get to walk closely with your son, and encourage him onwards.

Negative self stories...

Still, as I've said, if we're to help our sons build a better story, we need to understand what they've gone through. If your son has experienced a lot of teasing and put-downs, he very likely carries a negative self-story, and it could go back a long way. To get to its roots, you may need to go back, to perhaps before he even started boarding.

It's like this. Some time ago, I was asked to see a boy because of social difficulties in the dorm. He would get teased, particularly about his looks, and he'd lose it. He was in the vicious cycle. He couldn't get out on his own. And just recently he'd been having thoughts of self-harm, and even suicide.

He sat down, looking like he didn't want to be there. He said he was 'fine', and 'all was good'. He was in a rush to get the 'all clear' from me, so he could get on with getting on. He didn't like talking, he didn't like getting emotional, and he'd long-since turned his back on child-like openness and vulnerability.

Anyway, I held him there. I slowed him down, and simply liked him. After a few lame jokes and some connecting questions, he relaxed, and started talking properly.

Turns out, he'd been feeling terrible about himself for a long time. Always getting teased for his looks. I asked if he ever thought 'why me?', and with sudden tears, he said "All the time". He said, "I'm ugly". He described looking at family photographs, and feeling different from his family. And ... with floods of tears ... "a disappointment".

This is the painful turn towards healing. Going here gives us a proper base for a better story.

I think we underestimate how early and how cumulative hurt can be. On the surface, all may be 'fine', but there's a parallel underground sewer running through the course of a boy's life. A negative, self-destructive story about me. An inherent sense that there's something wrong with me.

I also think we underestimate how common this is. Beneath our confidence and our stories of success, lurk alternate 'bad' or 'deficient' self stories. This is why so many of us are anxious, and why we rail at criticism or perceived mistakes. As I say, we all yearn to be seen as a good person, and we fear being 'found out' for being bad.

So perhaps before you go there with your son, take a moment to work out your 'worst self' story, how it got there, and how it gets fed, even to this day. This will give you ways of talking with your son. And it means you can reassure him that he's not the only one – that in some or other way, all of us need liberation from stories of failure, guilt, and inadequacy.

Hold the bad story up to the light

Once our bad stories are out there, in the open, we realise they represent only *one part* of us – only one thread in the overall weave. Yes, we are flawed. Yet we are also fearfully and wonderfully made. And we are not yet done! There is more to come. This is robust self-esteem. I'm not 'all that'… and yet, watch this space! I'm coming, just watch me!

Talking through our bad stories also helps us to see the awful lies they contain. Take this boy. Deep inside, and for too long, he's carried the belief that his body-type is bad. Where does this message come from? What media has wound its way into his soul, telling him he is ugly? What are the social conventions that have made him compare himself, always for the worse, with his family and peers?

And how can he look at himself anew, afresh, and start to celebrate what is? There I sit, across the room from a young, very healthy, still-developing teen, and he hates his body! No. He has to look again. He has to realise what he's got and he has to start seeing what's possible. And from this day on, I want him to join the growing throng of young people who must resist the lies they hear 'out there' – from the always frowning, never satisfied, social media judge.

Strength in the weakness

A while ago I was talking with a boy who was being tormented by one of his dorm mates – a bigger, much stronger boy. We'd been talking for a while, so first-up we reviewed his coping strategies. A year in, he was far better at keeping his self-control; a major achievement on its own. Still, it was difficult for this boy to apply effective boundaries, and he had concerns about 'taking it further'.

What I did was to go to who the boy is – someone who isn't aggressive or violent. I spoke about this as one of his key attributes, and told him I admire him for it. I said we needed more men like him. At the same time, I also wanted him to stay open to his own emerging strength. This combination of who he is, with who he could be, really struck a chord. He looked away for a while and, with a half-smile, he started to imagine. This gangly, thoroughly adolescent boy started to envisage an authentic, yet much stronger version of himself. He imagined being able, in a few years' time, to properly confront bullies and draw a line in the sand – his way.

He's not there yet. In his own words, he's 'still weak'. But now he wants to start gym. He wants to grow himself, and with that, his social repertoire, including greater assertiveness.

Three stories…

So there you have three stories. One told by a middle-aged man, and two told by teenage boys. What do these stories show us?

- If you want to get to know someone, you need to hear his story.
- Stories consist of memorable moments, like beads on a necklace, running through our hands.
- My friend's story shows how durable these memorable moments can be.
- Hurtful or negative memories can form negative self stories, and these can block new or better stories.
- Invariably, our negative self stories remain unspoken.
- Realising we can change is inspiring.
- Imagining future moments creates hope and motivation.
- Imagining a new story *sets a positive cycle in place*: seeing future possibility makes us more motivated to act now; and what we do now can feed into our new future.
- Strengths and weaknesses can be deceptive. Right now, what looks like a weakness, could end up being a strength.

- On their own, our sons can't see the 'wood for the trees'. For a proper perspective on who they are, and who they're becoming, they need adult wisdom and guidance.

- Our sons find themselves in a particular culture, with powerful social rules about who they ought to be. Boys need to talk with an adult to properly see and critique these rules.

- Critiquing 'the way things are' can help your son to reclaim his authentic self, even as he goes about growing who he is, and accommodating to this culture.

Closing thoughts

One morning I made my way to one of the boarding schools in our area to meet with various members of staff. I arrived early, so for a while I waited and watched. The boys were on tea break – a time of laughter, relaxation, and … food! Off to one side, though, stood a junior, his head down, forlorn, standing in an area demarcated for transgressors.

Then I watched as a senior student walked towards this boy, holding a saucer on which he'd placed a generous slice of cake – someone's birthday, I realised. And I thought, "Wow! What a leader! What a good guy! How did he know to do this? Who taught him this big-picture ethic?"

My mind flicked back to my younger self. In these ways, I was clueless. I wouldn't have had the interior capacity to see what this senior boy saw. If others around me were punished or put-down, I wouldn't have thought to help them. And if I'd been teased or put-down, I wouldn't have known what to do. I reckon I could have done more, and been the happier for it, but I'd have needed guidance, back then, to be a better me. I was just too preoccupied, too defended, to see beyond my own adolescent anxieties and needs.

The other day I was talking with a boy who'd come through a season of peer difficulty, and he was starting to look back with insight. He said:

"I've never really thought about it, or put it into words… the big thing for me has been not trusting people".

There you have it. Putting something into words is the optimal way of thinking. By talking, this young man was able to see how 'not trusting' had become part of his survival strategy. Just think how much pain he's saving himself (and others) by realising this. With awareness, he can reassess his boundaries, and start opening up again to people he can and actually should trust. Just this change can give his story a completely different, far richer and healthier trajectory. He's set for a happier ending.

There's no healing of pain within the tight drum of a solitary mind. Relational pain can only be healed in and through relationship. You can provide this space for your son. Stand in his corner. Don't try and pull him out. Witness his pain. Love him. Remind him that he is good. And help him see which way to walk.

You are not finished yet. You are 'in the making'. You have the capacity to learn, mature, think, change and grow. You also have the freedom to stagnate, regress, constrict and lose your way. Which road will you take?

(Brian McLaren 'We make the road by walking')

References

Books cited:

Brown, B. (2015). *Daring Greatly: How the courage to be vulnerable transforms the way we live, love, parent, and lead.* Penguin Life: New York.

Dweck, C.S. (2007) *Mindset: The new psychology of success.* Ballantine Books: New York.

In her groundbreaking book, Carol Dweck explains that the growth mindset is "based on the belief that your basic qualities are things you can cultivate through effort".

Hartmann, T. (2019). *ADHD: A hunter in a farmer's world.* Healing Arts Press: Vermont.

Kalman, I. (2019). *Bullies to buddies. How to turn your enemies into friends.* Amazon Digital Services LLC-Kdp Print US.

McAdams, D.P. (1993). *The stories we live by: Personal myths and the making of the self.* The Guilford Press. New York.

McLaren, B. (2015). *We make the road by walking. A year-long quest for spiritual formation, reorientation, and activism.* Hodder: London.

Olweus, D. (2002). *Bullying at school.* Blackwell Publishing: Oxford.

Prinstein, M. (2017). *Popular: The power of likeability in a status obsessed world.* Penguin Audible.

Real, T. (2002). *How can I get through to you? Closing the intimacy gap between men and women.* Fireside: New York.

Siegel, D. (2004) *Parenting from the inside out. How a deeper self-understanding can help you raise children who thrive.* J.P. Tarcher: New York.

Potential benefits of Boarding Schools

Walker, S. P. (2017). *Steering with others in mind: The impacts of day and boarding education on the cognition of social agility and cohesion.* http://mind-world/education

Referring to the potential benefits and risks of boarding, the author notes that; *"the inference of this study is that boarding school pupils are more vulnerable, as well as more responsive, to the nuances of the social, emotional, and academic environment around them at school. The intensity of the experience provides both increased risk factors, as well as future protective factors to these pupils".*

The importance of social connection:

Anderman, L.H., & Freeman, T. (2004). Students' sense of belonging in school. In M.L. Maehr & PR Pintrich (Eds.), Advances in motivation and achievement: Vol 13.

Motivating Students, improving schools – The legacy of Carol Midgley (pp27-63). Greenwich, CT.

DeWall, N.C. & Bushman, B.J. (2011). *Social Acceptance and Rejection: The sweet and the bitter, vol. 20(4) 256-260. Current directions in Psychological Science.* https://doi.org/10.1177/0963721411417545

Hawkley, L.C., Cacioppo, J.T. (2010) Loneliness matters: a theoretical and empirical review of consequences and mechanisms. Annals of Behavioural Medicine, 40(2): 218-227.

The importance of belonging:

Allen, K.A., Kern, M.L., Rozek, C.S., McInereney, D., Slavich, G.M. (2022). Belonging: A review of conceptual issues, an integrative framework, and directions for future research. *Australian Journal of Psychology,* 73(1), 87-102. https://doi.org/10.1080/00049530.2021.1883409

The authors say that "a sense of belonging ... is a fundamental human need that predicts numerous mental, physical, social, economic and behavioural outcomes

Goodenow and Grady (1993) in Allen, Kelly; Kern, Margaret, L.; Vella-Broderick, Dianne; Hattie, John Walters, Lea (March 2018). "What schools need to know about Fostering School Belonging: A Meta-analysis" Educational Psychology Review. 30(1): 1-34.

The authors define belonging as: "the extent to which students feel personally accepted, respected, included and supported by others in the school environment".

Social connection and performance:

Benningfield, M.M, Potter, M.P., & Bostic, J. Q. (2015). Educational impacts of the social and emotional brain. *Child and Adolescent Psychiatric Clinics,* 24(2), 261-275.

Cacioppo, J.T., & Hawkley, L.C. (2009). Perceived social isolation and cognition. *Trends in Cognitive Sciences,* 13(10, 447-454.

Eather, N., Wade, L., Pankowiak, A. *et al.* The impact of sports participation on mental health and social outcomes in adults: a systematic review and the 'Mental Health through Sport' conceptual model: *Syst Rev* 12, 102 (2023). https://doi.org/10.1186/s13643-023-02264-8

These authors find that the "evidence indicates that participation in sport (community and elite) is related to better mental health, including improved psychological well-being (for example higher self-esteem and life satisfaction) and lower psychological ill-being (for example reduced levels of depression, anxiety, and stress) and improved social outcomes".

Katagami, E., Tsuchiya, H. (2016). Effects of social support on Athlete's Psychological well-being: The correlations between received support, perceived support, and personality. *Psychology* 7(13). DOI: 10.4236/psych.2016.713163

This study suggests that social support emerges as a key factor for both the well-being and performance of athletes.

Social connection and the body:

Nair, S. Sollers, J, Consedine D., Broadbent, E. (2015). Do slumped and upright postures affect stress responses? A randomized trial. Health Psychology, June, 34(6) 632-41.

Social rejection is pain (MacDonald, G.; Leary MR. (2005). "Why does social exclusion hurt? The relationship between social and physical pain". Psychological Bulletin. 131. (2) 202-223.

Cross, M.P, Acevedo, A.m., Leger, K.A., Pressman, S.D. How and why could smiling influence physical health? A conceptual review. Health Psychological Rev. 2023 Jun; 17(2):321-343. Doi:10.1080/17437199.2022.2052740. Epub 2022 Mar 23. PMID: 35285408.

The authors say that "studies consistently suggest that smiling may have a number of health-relevant benefits including beneficially impacting our physiology during acute stress, improved stress recovery, and reduced illness over time".

Steptoe, A., Owen, N., Kunz-Ebrecht, S.R., Brydon, L. (2004). Loneliness and neuroendocrine, cardiovascular, and inflammatory stress response in middle-aged men and women. Psycho neuroendocrinology. 29(5): 593-611.

Spiritual connection and mental health:

Michaelson, V.; King, N.; Smigeskas, K.; Dackeviciené, A.S.; Malinowska-Cieslik, M.; Patte, K.; Gardner, P; Inchley, J.; Pickett, W.HSBC Spiritual Health Writing Group. Establishing spirituality as an intermediary determinant of health among 42 843 children from eight countries. *Journal of Preventative Medicine.* 2024, Feb. 107846. DOI.10:1016/jypmed-2024Jan4PMID: 38181895.

This recent, and vast study involved over 42000 children, ages 11-15, from eight different countries. The study found that mental health was strongly and consistently buffered by connection with others, with nature, with the spiritual, and with the self, promoting a sense of meaning and purpose.

Iain McGilchrist is a psychiatrist, neuroscience researcher, philosopher, and literary scholar. In his recent, and significant book; *'The matter with things'*, McGilchrist emphasizes the vital importance of spiritual connection, arguing that relationships, including our relationship with a higher power or the cosmos, are primary to the things that are related. He suggests that spiritual connection is not just a matter of belief, but a fundamental aspect of human experience and well-being.

McGilchrist says that Religion is a key way of emphasising the importance of relationships. He writes: "A religious cast of mind sets the human being and human life in the widest context, reminding us of our duties to one another, and to the natural world that is our home; duties, however, that are founded in love and link us to the whole of existence. The world becomes ensouled. And we have a place in it once more."

See *'Understanding the McGilchrist worldview, eleven major premises discernible in The Matter with Things'*, by David Mcilroy, in Perspectiva, Jan 25, 2024.

www.ingramcontent.com/pod-product-compliance
Lightning Source LLC
Chambersburg PA
CBHW070815050426
42452CB00011B/2050